The Kids Book of
WORLD RELIGIONS

WRITTEN BY

Jennifer Glossop

ILLUSTRATED BY

John Mantha

KIDS CAN PRESS

Acknowledgments

Even those who belong to the same religion often disagree about its beliefs and history. What's more, scholars have argued for centuries about interpretations of sacred texts. Preparing this book, which covers so much in so small a space, was therefore truly challenging. I am most grateful to those who offered their wisdom and provided clarifications about their religions and those of others. These helpful people included Professor Julia Ching, Reverend Cheri di Novo, Rabbi Lawrence A. Englander, Theresa K. Gerson, Louise Johnston, Puneet Singh Kohli, Imam Ibrahim H. Malabari, Dr. Solomon A. Nigosian, Professor Willard G. Oxtoby, Eli Rubenstein, Kalakad S. Sathi, Reverend Dr. Phyllis Smyth, Rabbi Michael S. Stroh and Tak-Ling Terry Woo.

In addition to providing many of the photographs, my editor, Christine McClymont, made astute suggestions and patiently stayed the course through the long journey.
I hope that this book will provide an introduction to a topic that touches all of us and continues both to divide and to unite our world.

Photo Credits
Allan Griffin: 18, 22, 40, 44, 54, 58. **Jassie Khurana:** 16.
Christine McClymont: 21, 41, 43, 48, 53, 56, 59. **Brigitte Shapiro:** 34.

First paperback edition 2013

Published in Canada and the U.S. by Kids Can Press Ltd.
25 Dockside Drive, Toronto, ON M5A 0B5

Kids Can Press is a Corus Entertainment Inc. company

www.kidscanpress.com

Edited by Christine McClymont
Designed by Julia Naimska

Printed in Malaysia in 12/2021 by Times Offset Malaysia

CM 03 0 9 8 7 6 5 4 3 2 1
CM PA 13 0 9 8

Library and Archives Canada Cataloguing in Publication

Glossop, Jennifer
The kids book of world religions / written by Jennifer Glossop ;
illustrated by John Mantha.

Includes index.
ISBN 1-55074-959-5 (bound).   ISBN 978-1-55453-981-9 (pbk.)

1. Religions — Juvenile literature. I. Mantha, John II. Title.

BL92.G58 2003   j291   C2002-902603-2

Kids Can Press gratefully acknowledges that the land on which our office is located is the traditional territory of many nations, including the Mississaugas of the Credit, the Anishnabeg, the Chippewa, the Haudenosaunee and the Wendat peoples, and is now home to many diverse First Nations, Inuit and Métis peoples.

We thank the Government of Ontario, through Ontario Creates; the Ontario Arts Council; the Canada Council for the Arts; and the Government of Canada for supporting our publishing activity.

CONTENTS

WHAT IS RELIGION?

Human beings are curious creatures. We like to ask questions. We like to find out why things are the way they are and how things work. Long ago, people told stories to explain things like the seasons and the weather. We call these stories myths. One ancient Greek myth explained that it got cold in winter because a beautiful woman was trapped in the underworld for part of the year. Another myth said that lightning was a weapon the Gods threw at each other.

Today, science gives us answers to lots of questions. It tells us why leaves change color in the fall and what causes thunder and lightning. But there are other questions that science doesn't answer — especially big questions about the meaning and purpose of life.

BIG QUESTIONS

- Is there a God?
- Can I talk to God?
- How was the world created?
- What happens when people die?
- How should I live my life?
- Why do bad things happen?
- How can we celebrate special times?
- What makes some objects and places special?

Religions offer answers to these big questions. Sometimes the answers — or teachings — of one religion are very similar to those of others, and sometimes they are different.

When people belong to one religion, they usually agree with its teachings. People may be born into a religion or choose it later in life. Belonging to a religion helps people feel part of a community that shares their beliefs.

Most religions encourage people to be aware of something beyond everyday human life. Even though people can't see or understand this larger reality, they can feel a sense of wonder about it.

Athena

Ancient Religions

Many ancient religions taught that powerful, invisible beings lived all around us. These Gods or spirits lived in trees or streams, or they dwelt in the sky and looked down to see what human beings were doing. People tried to talk to these Gods and ask them for help. Sometimes they gave the Gods food or other gifts. They believed that if the Gods were pleased, they would provide good weather, a safe hunt or healthy children. The ancient Greeks prayed to the Goddess Athena (above) for her wisdom.

The Golden Temple of the Sikhs

Shiva, one of the Hindu Gods

Muslim pilgrims in Mecca

RELIGIONS TRY TO ANSWER THE BIG QUESTIONS

Is there a God?

Human beings have often felt that there is someone or something in the universe greater than themselves. They usually call this greater power God.

Most religions teach that a God or Gods exist. Some, such as Judaism, Christianity and Islam, teach that there is only one God, who is the creator of all things. A Creator god is also part of many Indigenous religions in North America, but the Creator may be joined by other spirits as well.

Some religions teach that there are many Gods who are all part of one divine being. For example, many Hindus believe in thousands of Gods who are part of one God, Brahman. Many Buddhists and Jains, on the other hand, do not believe in a God. Confucianism is more concerned with teaching people how to act in this life.

Can I talk to God?

People pray as a way of speaking to God. A prayer may say "thank you" or "forgive me" or "please help me." Some prayers simply say who God is or praise God's greatness and goodness.

Worship usually involves a way of recognizing the greatness of God or of something beyond human beings. Prayer is often part of worship. At worship services, people gather together to pray aloud, chant or sing, and to listen to readings from holy books. They may kneel, sit or stand.

Sometimes they hear a talk called a sermon. Meditation — sitting still and focusing one's thoughts — can also be part of worship.

The places where people worship may be called churches, synagogues, gurdwaras or temples. They may be large and fancy or simple and plain. Services may occur every day, once a week or any time at all. Sometimes men and women have different places to stand or sit. People often cover their heads or take off their shoes to show respect for the place of worship.

Jews praying at the Western Wall in Jerusalem

Mother Teresa

The Good and the Bad

People do many things in the name of their religion, some of which are bad. Some people dislike others simply because of the God or Gods they believe in or don't believe in. What is worse, people have fought and killed each other over religion.

People do many good things in the name of religion as well. All over the world, religious people feed the poor, teach others, speak out for social justice and take care of sick and dying people. Religious people have also created some of the world's most beautiful music, art, buildings and gardens.

A Zoroastrian Tower of Silence

Indigenous Australian peoples celebrating Dreamtime

What happens when people die?

Religions usually have teachings about whether or not there is another life after we die. Some religions say that we have souls. A soul is an invisible part of a person that is different from the body but a basic part of the person. Some religions teach that our souls go to heaven if we have been good or to hell if we have been bad. Others say that our souls come back after death in another form — as a different person or as an animal. Some religions claim that people who die become spirits or ghosts and continue to live among us.

A traditional Chinese funeral ceremony

How was the world created?

Most religions tell a story about how the world was created. The Bible of Judaism and Christianity says that God created the universe and all the plants, animals and people in six days, then rested on the seventh day.

The people of the Hopi Nation in the American Southwest tell a creation story about four worlds — this one on the earth and three cave worlds below it. The people of long ago lived in darkness and difficulty until they were led out by Spider Grandmother and two brothers. On their journey from one world to the next, the people received many gifts and learned special ceremonies.

How should I live my life?

All religions tell us that we should treat other people as we would like to be treated ourselves. To put it simply, if we don't want to be hit, then we shouldn't hit others. This teaching is often called the Golden Rule. Most religions also urge people to help those less fortunate than themselves. Some religions have rules about what to eat and drink. Religions often expect people to dress modestly, and some have distinctive clothes for men and women or for religious leaders.

Some people join special religious groups so they can devote part or all of their lives to their religion. Buddhist monks and Hindu holy men give up all their possessions and depend on others to take care of them.

Most religions have leaders who teach the people about their faith and perform the most important religious ceremonies. In some religions, anyone can do these things. In others, only those who have studied and made special promises can do so.

Buddhist nuns in North America

Holy books, which most religions have, give rules for daily living. They may also contain prayers and songs, the history of the group's beliefs and the words used for ceremonies. These sacred texts can sometimes be based on the sayings of one person such as Jesus (in the New Testament of the Christian Bible) or Lao Tzu (in the Tao Te Ching).

Why do bad things happen?

Understanding why bad things happen is not easy. Even more puzzling for believers in a just God is why good people often suffer and bad people may not. Zoroastrianism says that good is constantly fighting against evil in the universe, and evil sometimes wins. Other religions say that people are free to do what they want, and sometimes they choose to do bad things.

Lao Tzu, founder of Taoism

Does Everyone Believe in a God?

Not everyone believes in a God or follows a religion. Many millions of people are non-believers.

People who do not believe in a God are called atheists. Throughout history, many thinkers and scientists have been atheists. Some say that there is no proof that God exists. Others believe that people have simply made up religions over time. Still others think that religions keep people from being free.

Agnostics believe there is no proof that God exists, but that it is possible. Some agnostics take part in religions. While they doubt the existence of a God, they accept other teachings of the religion and value its traditions.

Christian children celebrating Christmas

Why are some objects and places special?

Most religions give some objects and places a special meaning. The cross is a symbol that reminds Christians of the death of Jesus. The symbol of a crescent moon and star appears on Muslim flags. Mount Fuji in Japan is sacred to the followers of Shinto, and the Ganges River is sacred to Hindus. Places where the central person of the religion was born or where important events occurred are also held in great honor. Followers of a religion make trips, called pilgrimages, to visit these places.

The Ganges River, sacred to Hindus

How can we celebrate special times?

Most religions have special ceremonies to mark and celebrate the major events of our lives. Birth and marriage ceremonies are happy occasions. When someone dies, a funeral is held to remember and honor the person and to bring some comfort to the grieving family and friends. The time when a child or adult joins a religion is often celebrated as well.

Religious festivals can be fun as well as serious. Most religions have special times of the year when people get together, sing songs, enjoy good food and give one another presents. Often people give to the poor as well. Some holy days (this is where the word "holidays" comes from) recall unhappy times in the past. On Good Friday, Christians remember the death of Jesus. The Jewish holy day Yom Kippur is a time when people ask forgiveness from those they have hurt and think about how they can be better in the future.

The Calendar Connection

The calendar used in most parts of the world today is based on Christianity. It counts the years from the date on which Jesus was thought to have been born. Ten years after his birth was A.D. 10 (for Anno Domini, the year of Our Lord), while ten years before was 10 B.C. (for Before Christ).

Other religions start counting the years from different events. The Islamic calendar starts from the year in which Muhammad went to Medina.

The lunar calendar, based on the moon, is used by Jews, Muslims, followers of Chinese religions and many others. Each month lasts from one new moon to the next.

This book follows the recent custom of using the initials C.E. for Common Era (instead of A.D.) and B.C.E. for Before the Common Era (instead of B.C.).

SYMBOLS OF WORLD RELIGIONS

Hinduism

 This is the written form of the sacred sound "Om" or "Aum." Hindus often chant it as they meditate.

Buddhism

 Buddha spoke about an Eightfold Path to living well and becoming enlightened. The eight-spoked wheel represents this Path.

Sikhism

 The circle symbolizes the eternal God, while the two outer swords show that Sikhs are ready to defend truth and justice.

Jainism

 The upright hand reminds Jains to act wisely and peacefully. The word for "non-violence" is written on the palm.

Judaism

 The menorah, a seven-branched candlestick, lit the ancient Temple of Jerusalem and represents the Jewish people today.

Christianity

 Jesus Christ died on a cross. For Christians, the cross symbolizes his death and resurrection and his promise of eternal life.

Islam

 As the star guides the traveler, so Muslims are guided by Islam. The crescent moon is a symbol of new beginnings.

Zoroastrianism

 Ahura Mazda is the supreme creator spirit in the Zoroastrian religion. This ancient image of him was carved in Iran.

Baha'i

 The Baha'i faith teaches that there is one God for all people and all religions are one. The interlocking triangles represent that unity.

Taoism/Confucianism

 This symbol shows how the forces of yin — dark and heavy — and yang — light and airy — balance each other.

Shinto

 Shinto shrines have a gate like this one, called a torii. It invites people to enter and worship.

HOW THIS BOOK IS ORGANIZED

The major religions included in this book started in various parts of the world. The Map of World Religions on pages 10 and 11 shows how religions have spread to other countries and continents.

The Glossary on page 63 gives definitions of special words used to describe religions.

Religions from India

Hinduism, Buddhism, Sikhism and Jainism began in India. They all teach reincarnation — the belief that after death people are reborn into another life on earth. Hinduism is the oldest of these four religions, dating back thousands of years.

Religions from the Middle East

The three main religions from the Middle East — Judaism, Christianity and Islam — trace their history back to one common ancestor, Abraham. These religions are also linked by their belief in one God.

Zoroastrianism is an ancient Middle Eastern religion, while Baha'i is only 150 years old.

Religions from East Asia

Taoism and Confucianism come from China and focus on how people can live a good life. Shinto, Japan's oldest religion, is based on the worship of spirits.

Religions from Other Continents

The religions that began in Africa, Australia and North America are very ancient. They teach people about a supernatural world of spirits who affect the lives of human beings.

MAP OF WORLD RELIGIONS

This map shows how the major religions have spread around the world. The colors indicate the religion or religions followed by the largest number of people in that area. In most places, there are also smaller numbers of people who believe in other faiths or do not follow any religion, and others, including Indigenous Peoples, who practice their cultures' traditional spirituality along with that of another faith.

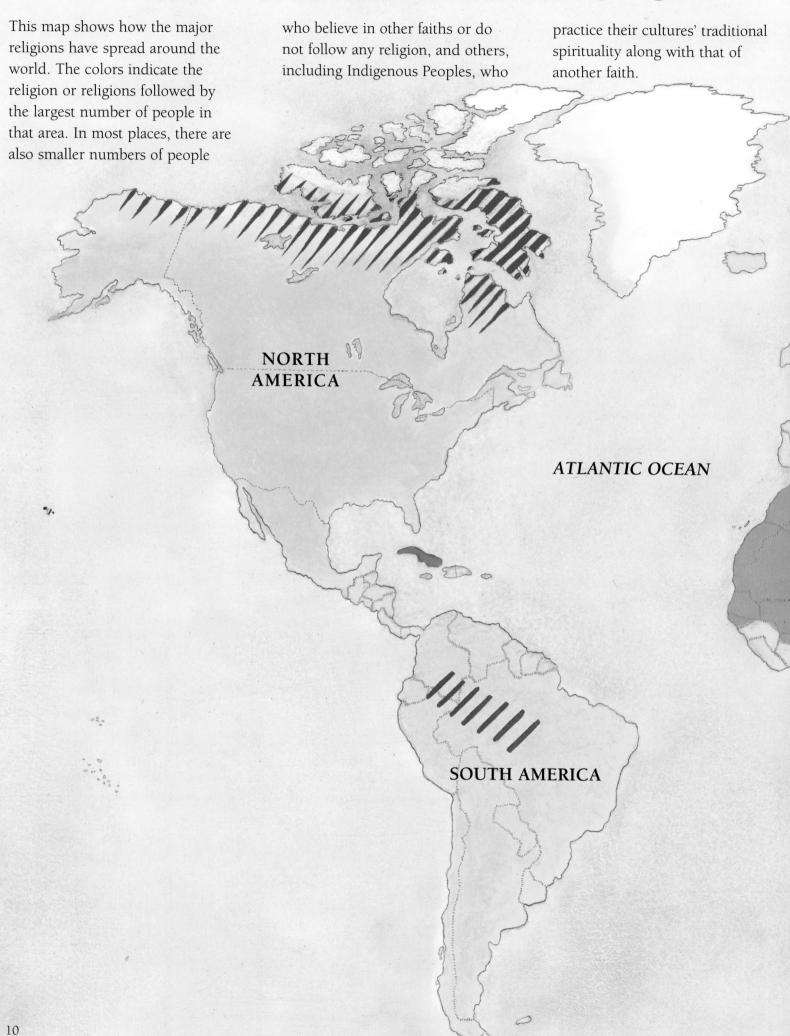

NORTH AMERICA

ATLANTIC OCEAN

SOUTH AMERICA

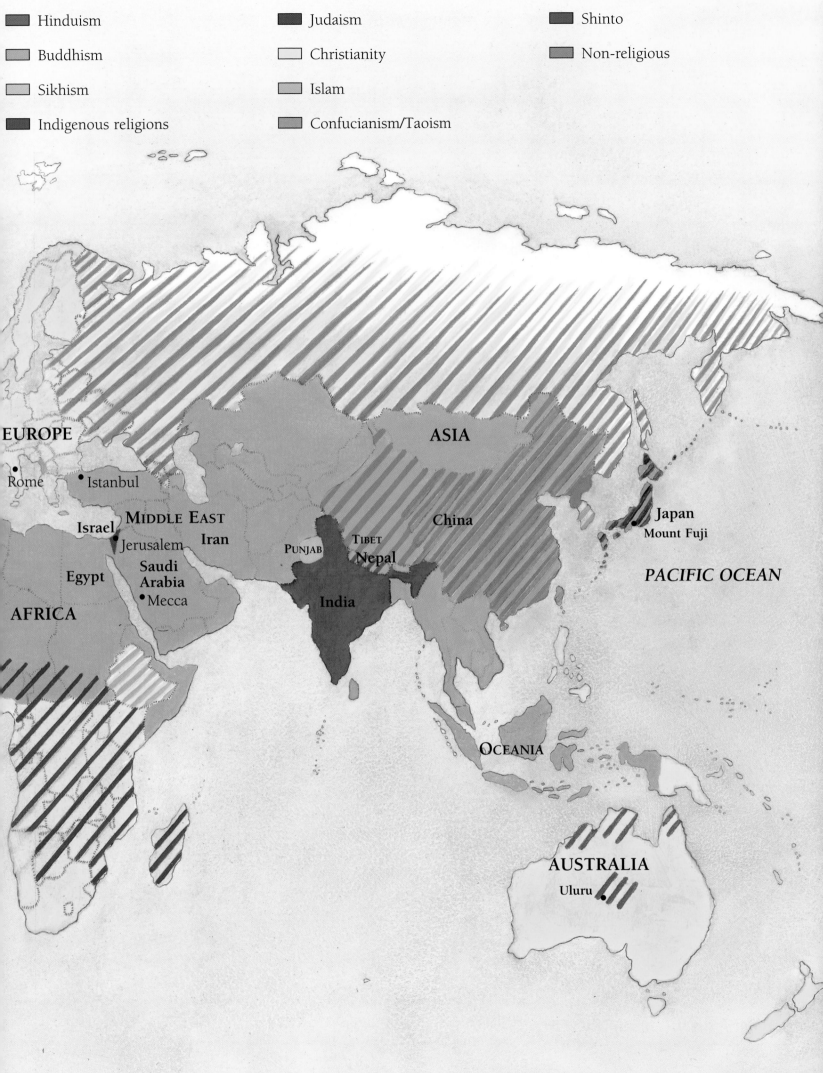

Hinduism	Judaism	Shinto
Buddhism	Christianity	Non-religious
Sikhism	Islam	
Indigenous religions	Confucianism/Taoism	

EUROPE

• Rome

• Istanbul

ASIA

MIDDLE EAST

Israel

Iran

China

Jerusalem

PUNJAB

TIBET

Japan

Egypt

Saudi
Arabia

Nepal

Mount Fuji

• Mecca

India

PACIFIC OCEAN

AFRICA

OCEANIA

AUSTRALIA

Uluru •

HINDUISM

We sometimes see pictures of people bathing in the River Ganges in India. These people are Hindus, and they believe the river is holy. Most Hindus live in India, and most people in India — eight out of ten — are Hindu.

The name "Hindu" originally referred to the people of the Indus River in northern India. Europeans gave the name Hindu to the religion of the people who lived there as well. Some Hindus call their religion *sanatana dharma* (pronounced sa-na-ta-na DAR-ma), which means eternal teaching or law.

Hinduism is very old — at least three thousand years — and has changed over time. Hinduism is a religion and a way of life. It teaches that everything we do has religious meaning. People's good or bad actions decide in what form they will be reborn in their next life on Earth.

TEACHINGS AND BELIEFS

Some Hindus believe that one supreme spirit, Brahman, is the origin of everything and is everywhere and in everything. The part of Brahman that lives in a person is called the *atman*, or soul.

Hindus may worship Brahman as a divine being who has no shape or form, or they may worship one or many of the hundreds of Hindu Gods and Goddesses. All of nature is part of Brahman, as are all the Gods and Goddesses. The three main Gods are Brahma, Vishnu and Shiva.

Brahma is the creator. In pictures, he is shown with four arms and four faces. He sits on a swan or a lotus flower. His wife is Sarasvati, the Goddess of learning and music.

Vishnu holds a conch shell, a discus, a club and a lotus flower.

Vishnu is the preserver. He enters the world when evil threatens to overcome good. The forms that he appears in are called *avatars*. Hindus believe that Vishnu has appeared on earth nine times so far, sometimes as a man and sometimes as an animal, and that he will appear one more time. The stories of Vishnu's two best-loved avatars, Rama and Krishna, are told in *epics* (long poems that tell stories). In pictures, Vishnu is blue like the sky because he is everywhere. His wife is Lakshmi, the Goddess of wealth and good luck.

Showing three of his four faces, Brahma, one of the Hindu Gods, sits on a lotus flower.

QUICK FACTS

Followers: *1 billion*

Locations: *India, Nepal, South Africa, Europe, North America, Southeast Asia*

Gods: *Brahman (supreme spirit) and thousands of Gods and Goddesses*

Scriptures: *Vedas, Upanishads, epic poems*

Places of worship: *temples*

Religious leaders: *brahmins (priests), sadhus (holy men), gurus (teachers)*

Major festivals: *Diwali, Holi*

To Hindus, the waters of the Ganges River in northern India hold special powers.

Shiva is the destroyer, but he also creates. He crushes evil so that good can follow. He caught the waters of the Ganges River in his hair as they flowed from heaven so that they would not harm the earth. Shiva is also called the Lord of the Dance. His wife sometimes appears as Parvati, who is kind and protective. At other times, she appears as Durga, the warrior Goddess who rides a tiger, or as Kali, who wears a necklace of skulls.

The Caste System

In the past, Hindu society was divided into several levels or *castes*. People could not change their caste during their lifetime. Belonging to an upper or lower caste decided their job, where they lived and whom they married. Today, the caste system is not followed as rigidly as it once was, but it can still affect people's opportunities in life.

Ganesh, the son of Shiva and Parvati, has an elephant head. Hindus pray to this God for good luck when they begin new projects.

Shiva is the God who destroys but also creates.

Reincarnation

Hindus believe that the soul does not die with the body. Instead, the soul casts off the body as if it were old clothes. Then the soul is reborn into another life. The law of *karma* rules this process, which is called reincarnation. According to karma, everything a person does has an effect in his or her next life. If a person does good deeds, he or she will be reborn as a person in a better position. But if a person acts badly, he or she might return as an animal.

Eventually, after hundreds or thousands of lives, the individual soul can break free of karma and be reunited with the supreme spirit. This release from the cycle of reincarnation is called *moksha*.

SCRIPTURES

The Vedas and the Upanishads

Hinduism has many sacred texts or scriptures. The oldest are the four Vedas. Hindus believe that they are God's revelations. Although they existed several thousand years ago, the Vedas were not written down until about six hundred years ago. Until then, priests memorized the words and taught them to the next generation. The Vedas are written in Sanskrit, an ancient language no longer in everyday use.

The Vedas contain hymns praising the ancient Gods and Goddesses. They also tell stories, such as this creation story: In the beginning, Purusha, the cosmic man, sacrificed himself to create the universe. The moon was made from his mind, the sun from his eye. Humans were created from his body: the priests from his face, the warriors and nobles from his arms, the merchants and farmers from his thighs and the servants from his feet.

The Upanishads (pronounced oo-PA-nee-shads) are also very old texts, although not as old as the Vedas. They contain important teachings about how to live and what happens when people die.

The Story of Rama and Sita

Two epic poems are important to Hinduism. The Ramayana tells the story of Rama, one of the avatars of Vishnu. When Prince Rama was banished from his kingdom, he went

Prince Rama, with his wife, Sita, and Hanuman the monkey God, faces his enemies in the forest.

to live in the forest with his wife, Sita, and his brother Lakshmana.

Sita was captured by the evil demon Ravana and taken to the island of Lanka. With the help of his brother and the monkey God, Hanuman, Rama built a bridge and fought many battles to rescue Sita. The people welcomed Rama and Sita when they returned to their kingdom. Each year, the festival of Diwali celebrates their return.

The Story of Arjuna and Krishna

The second epic, the Mahabharata, is the longest in the world. One part of it, the Bhagavad-Gita, tells the story of a warrior named Arjuna who is preparing to fight a great battle.

Arjuna worries that he may have to kill his enemies, some of whom are his teachers and relatives. He explains this to his chariot driver, who is actually Krishna, another avatar of Vishnu. Krishna teaches Arjuna about his duty as a warrior. He explains that since the soul does not die, Arjuna should not grieve over the dead.

Then Krishna teaches him the three paths that lead to a release from the cycle of reincarnation. They are knowledge, good actions and devotion to a God or Goddess. This is one of the most important lessons of Hinduism.

Life Is Sacred

Because Hinduism teaches that all human and animal life is sacred, many Hindus are vegetarians. Even those who eat meat will not eat beef. They honor the cow as especially holy. In India, cows are allowed to wander freely.

WORSHIP

Hindus worship at home and at temples. Daily worship takes place in the home, where an image of a favorite God or Goddess resides in a shrine. Children and their families worship at the shrine, offering prayers and gifts of food or flowers. They also burn incense and light small lamps.

In India, even the smallest village has at least one temple. An ancient banyan tree often grows nearby. The temple is usually the home of one God or Goddess, and an image of that God is kept in the center of the temple. When people visit, they walk around the shrine, praying, singing and offering gifts to the God. The priest bathes and clothes the image during the worship service. At the end of the service, worshipers receive gifts of fruit or flowers to represent the grace of the God.

Religious Leaders

Brahmins are priests who perform temple and religious services, visit homes, figure out horoscopes and perform weddings and other rituals.

Sadhus are holy men who have given up worldly pleasures. Some wear yellow robes and practice spiritual and physical exercises called *yoga*.

Gurus are religious teachers who may be sadhus as well.

Hindu sadhus, like this man, depend on the charity of others.

Four Stages of Life

Hinduism teaches that the ideal life has four stages:
1. a student of traditional literature
2. a householder, married, looking after children and responsible to society
3. a thinker, contemplating spiritual matters
4. a wandering monk who has given up family life

A girl worships at the shrine of the Goddess Sarasvati in her home.

MAHATMA GANDHI

Mahatma Gandhi, who was born in India in 1869, believed deeply in non-violence. His ideas were influenced by the Hindu belief that all life is sacred. Gandhi developed methods such as peaceful demonstrations and hunger strikes to protest injustice. Under his leadership, India was freed from British rule in 1947. Gandhi was assassinated in 1948. He has inspired many other activists, including Martin Luther King, Jr., the American civil-rights leader.

In the courtyard of Lingaraj temple in India, men gather for ritual duties. Hindu temples have a source of water where priests can bathe before worship.

Hindu Goals in Life

- Doing your duty towards God, society, family and yourself (*dharma*)
- Earning and spending money for the good of family and community
- Enjoying the good things in life
- Attaining release from the cycle of reincarnation by doing good deeds

The Sacred Thread Ceremony

Upper-caste boys take part in a ceremony that marks the beginning of their religious education and their social responsibilities. The boy bathes and dresses in new clothes. A priest performs a ritual and then gives the boy a white cotton thread that he wears over his left shoulder, across his chest and under his right arm. He promises to fulfill his duties to God and his family and learns a *mantra* (sacred phrase) that he will repeat every day from then on — "I meditate on the brilliance of the sun; may it light my mind."

SACRED PLACES

Hindus believe that some places are especially holy, and that visiting them brings a person closer to release from the cycle of reincarnation. Among these places are certain cities, temples and mountains. The most sacred river is the Ganges, which is believed to have flowed down from heaven to earth. Bathing in the Ganges, preferably at dawn, washes away the effect of bad actions.

MARKING SPECIAL EVENTS
Childhood

Hindu rituals begin even before birth, when parents-to-be pray for the health of their baby. At birth, friends and family pray for the baby's long life, learning and good fortune. Other childhood ceremonies include a naming ceremony (usually at twelve days old), first feeding of solid food (at six months), a boy's first haircut (usually at one year old), and the first birthday.

Yoga

People practice many kinds of yoga. Some involve meditation and others physical exercise. This is the lotus position in the practice of *hatha yoga*. Many Hindu Gods are portrayed sitting in this position.

The sacred thread ceremony marks a new stage in a Hindu boy's life.

Weddings

Traditionally, a Hindu couple's parents arrange their marriage. Parents often prefer that the bride and groom come from the same area, belong to the same caste and speak the same language. They may also check the young people's horoscopes to make sure they suit each other.

A Hindu couple exchange flowers at their wedding.

For the wedding, the bride wears special jewelry and a red *sari* (a long piece of fabric wrapped around the body). Often her hands and feet are decorated. She and the groom join hands and walk around a sacred fire, praying to God. They take seven steps that represent food, strength, prosperity, happiness, children, the enjoyment of pleasures, and a lifelong friendship.

Funerals

After a person dies, the family cremates the body, traditionally on a large bonfire. When the flames are lit, mourners say prayers for the peace of the departed soul. The ashes are scattered on the Ganges, if possible, or on other rivers.

At the festival of Diwali, families light lamps called diyas.

FESTIVALS

There are many celebrations and festivals during the Hindu calendar, which is based on the moon.

Holi

Holi is a popular spring festival in some parts of India. Because Holi recalls the pranks that Krishna played as a young man, the celebrations are full of high spirits. People light bonfires, play tricks and throw colored water on each other. At the end of the day, they change clothes and visit friends, and order is restored.

At Holi, children throw colored water and powder on each other.

Diwali

In India and around the world, Hindu children look forward to Diwali. This festival takes place in the fall between October 15 and November 15, when the sky is at its darkest before a new moon. Children have a holiday from school. They also receive presents and eat delicious food. Families light lamps called *diyas* to welcome Prince Rama and his wife, Sita, home after their defeat of the evil demon Ravana.

Diwali is also a time to welcome the Goddess Lakshmi and ask her to drive away misfortune. To honor her and invite her in, doors and windows are opened, the house is cleaned and everyone puts on clean clothes. At the end of the last day of Diwali, children enjoy a fireworks display.

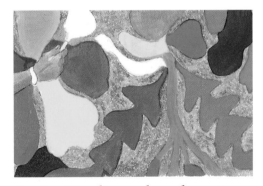

During Diwali, people make patterns called rangoli in front of their homes and household shrines to attract Lakshmi, Goddess of wealth.

BUDDHISM

 The statues below give three different images of one man — Siddhartha Gautama, the founder of Buddhism. In the first, he is trying to starve himself to reach enlightenment — a joyful state of perfect understanding. In the second, he has reached enlightenment. In the third, he is lying peacefully on his side, shortly before he died.

Siddhartha is called the Buddha, or Awakened One, because he reached enlightenment. He taught his followers how they, too, could reach this state.

A person reaches enlightenment on his or her own. But the steps toward it involve caring for other people and the earth.

Siddhartha when starving himself

Statue of a plump, smiling Buddha

A reclining Buddha in Thailand

THE LIFE OF THE BUDDHA

Siddhartha Gautama was born about 500 B.C.E. near the present-day border between Nepal and India. It is said that before Siddhartha was born, his mother had a dream. Priests interpreted the dream to mean that Siddhartha would be either a great ruler or a spiritual leader. His father wanted him to be a ruler, as he himself was, and he sheltered the boy and gave him everything he wanted.

Siddhartha was a happy and caring child who grew up knowing nothing about the world outside the gardens of his father's home. As a young man, he married and had a son.

When he was twenty-nine, Siddhartha finally ventured outside. There he saw a sick man. He had never seen illness before and was troubled by the man's pain. Next he saw an old man and then a dead person being carried to his funeral. He asked his servant to explain these strange sights, and the servant told him that all people get sick, grow old and die.

Siddhartha also saw a Hindu holy man and was amazed that the man could be so calm when surrounded by such misery. He decided to follow the holy man's example. He said good-bye to his family. Then he cut off his hair and threw away his clothes. He put on a simple robe and began a new life.

Buddhist monks shave their heads as Siddhartha did.

Siddhartha's Search for Wisdom

For six years, Siddhartha wandered and listened to holy men. He even tried to stop eating as a way to achieve wisdom. Instead, he became thin and ill. Deciding that starving himself was not the way, he accepted a meal from a woman who took pity on him.

Later, he sat cross-legged under a tree and meditated. During the night, Mara, the Lord of the Senses, sent visions to distract and terrify him. But Siddhartha defeated Mara. He reached enlightenment and realized the Four Noble Truths. From then on, he was called the Buddha, meaning Enlightened One.

Five friends joined the Buddha. He told them what he had learned — that too much is not good, but neither is too little. Instead, people should follow the Middle Path, which he called the Eightfold Path.

After his first sermon, the five men became the Buddha's first *disciples*, or followers. They and others became monks and nuns and formed a community, the *sangha*. Among the many people who joined were the Buddha's family.

The Buddha continued teaching until he was an old man. He died at the age of eighty, asking his followers not to be sad. All things change, he told them.

The Buddha reached enlightenment while sitting under a bodhi tree. Later he told his five friends what he had learned.

The Wheel of Dharma has a spoke for each step of the Eightfold Path (see page 20).

The Compassionate Life

The Buddha taught his followers to be generous and compassionate toward other people. In addition, he taught five rules, also called the Five Precepts.
1. Don't harm living things.
2. Don't take what is not given to you.
3. Don't misuse the senses.
4. Don't lie to yourself or others.
5. Don't drink alcohol or take drugs.

QUICK FACTS

Followers: 500 million

Locations: Sri Lanka, Thailand, Myanmar, Cambodia, Vietnam, Bhutan, Tibet, Korea, Mongolia, Japan, China, Taiwan, Europe, North America

Major branches: Theravada, Mahayana

Teacher/Founder: Siddhartha Gautama (the Buddha)

Scriptures: Tripitaka, Mahayana scriptures

Places of worship: shrines, temples and monasteries

Religious leaders: monks and nuns; lamas

Major festivals: Birth, death and enlightenment of Buddha

TEACHINGS AND BELIEFS

The Buddha taught that all things change. Some things change quickly. Others change slowly. After a leaf turns brown and falls, it decays and becomes part of a new plant. Over millions of years, mountains slowly rise, then are worn down into sand. A baby becomes a child, then a teenager, then an adult. If we want things to remain the same, we are sure to be disappointed. If we desire things — money, fame, pleasure — we also suffer from their loss.

The Buddha agreed with the Hindu teaching that everything that happens is caused by something else. This law of cause and effect is called *karma*. Good actions and thoughts produce good karma, and bad ones produce bad karma.

Buddhists believe in rebirth, but they do not believe in a permanent, unchanging soul. Everything changes, including the parts that make up a person. After death, these parts dissolve and come together in a new person. To Buddhists, life is like a fire. It has a shape but is constantly changing.

By following the Eightfold Path, a person may reach enlightenment, as the Buddha did. In this state, called *nirvana*, a person is freed from attachment to this world and from reincarnation.

In some countries, children can become Buddhist monks. These boys are studying at a monastery in Myanmar (formerly Burma).

RELIGIOUS WAYS

Like the early followers of the Buddha, who shaved their heads and gave up everything they owned, some Buddhists leave their everyday lives and join monasteries. They depend on others to give them food, which they collect in bowls. In monasteries, monks and nuns meditate and teach. Buddhists visit monasteries for special occasions and on festival days.

Buddhist homes have a shrine that contains a statue of the Buddha, candles, flowers and incense. Family members meditate in front of the shrine. Everyone tries to meditate twice a day.

The Four Noble Truths

- Life involves suffering and sorrow.
- The reason we suffer is that we want things for ourselves. We don't want things to change and yet they do.
- Suffering can end when we reduce selfishness.
- The cure for suffering is the Eightfold Path.

The Eightfold Path

The Buddha taught that the cure for suffering involves eight steps:
- Right view — Understand the Buddha's teachings (called *dharma*).
- Right thought — Think about others, not yourself.
- Right speech — Tell the truth, say helpful things.
- Right action — Do things that are kind and thoughtful.
- Right work — Do jobs that help others and do no harm.
- Right effort — Try to follow the right path.
- Right mindfulness — Be aware of your thoughts and actions.
- Right concentration — Focus your thoughts.

Buddhist travelers leave prayer flags on this mountain in Tibet.

The Three Jewels

The Buddha's followers asked him for protection and comfort, and he gave them the Three Jewels in which they could take refuge: "I go to the Buddha for refuge. I go to the dharma [teaching] for refuge. I go to the sangha [community] for refuge." Buddhists repeat these words in front of shrines at monasteries.

SCRIPTURES

The Three Baskets

After the Buddha died, his followers collected his teachings and memorized them. Centuries later his words were written down on palm leaves and placed in three baskets. They are called the Tripitaka or Three Baskets. The Three Baskets are (1) the teachings of the Buddha, (2) the monastic rules and (3) the Buddha's philosophy. The main branches of Buddhism — Theravada and Mahayana — accept these books. Mahayana has other sacred books as well.

BRANCHES OF BUDDHISM

As the Buddha's followers traveled, they were influenced by the beliefs of people in other lands such as Sri Lanka, China and Japan.

Theravada Buddhism

Of the many older forms of Buddhism, only Theravada remains. It encourages its followers to become monks and nuns. In Theravada countries such as Sri Lanka and Thailand, many people — including boys and old men — join monasteries. Their goal is to become an *arhat*, a person who has attained enlightenment and will not return to worldly life. Not everyone reaches this goal, and many people stay in monasteries for only a short time.

Mahayana Buddhism

In the first century C.E., a new form of Buddhism developed, called Mahayana. It teaches that everyone can attain enlightenment and become a *bodhisattva* (pronounced bow-dee-SAT-va). These people have reached nirvana but choose to stay in the world and help others, as the Buddha did.

Buddhist temples in Thailand, like this one in Bangkok, often contain cruel-looking giants who act as guardians to keep away evil spirits.

• Pure Land Buddhism

Pure Land Buddhism is one of the most popular forms of Mahayana Buddhism in eastern Asia, especially China and Japan. Pure Land Buddhists believe that people who have faith in the Buddha Amitabha (pronounced ah-me-TA-ba) will be born in the Western Land of Bliss. (Buddhists believe in many buddhas in addition to Siddhartha, who is sometimes called the Buddha Gautama.)

The most popular bodhisattva (enlightened person) is Avalokitesvara (pronounced ah-vah-loki-TASH-vera), called Kuan-yin in China and Kannon in Japan.

• Vajrayana Buddhism

Around 700 C.E., Mahayana Buddhism came to Tibet, a mountainous country between China and India. There it became known as Vajrayana Buddhism. Until recently, religion played an important part in the lives of the Tibetan people. Many lived as monks, with boys as young as eight years old joining monasteries.

Religious leaders are called *lamas*, Tibetan for guru. Some lamas are said to be reincarnations of previous lamas. When a lama dies, the monks search for the child in whom the former lama has been reincarnated.

The garden of Tofukuji Temple in Kyoto, Japan, is a place for meditation. Every morning, a Zen monk rakes the sand into wavy shapes around the islands of moss and mountains of rock.

◆ PROFILE ◆

DALAI LAMA

The Dalai Lama is the head of the main branch of Tibetan Buddhism. There have been fourteen Dalai Lamas. The first, who lived in the 1400s, was believed to be the bodhisattva Avalokitesvara in human form. Each Dalai Lama since has been seen as a reincarnation of the previous one.

The current Dalai Lama was born in 1935 in China. As a child, he showed who he was by identifying objects that had belonged to the previous Dalai Lama. He was enthroned in Tibet in 1940. He acted as a religious and political leader until 1950, when the Chinese took over Tibet. In 1959, the Dalai Lama and thousands of his followers escaped to India. In 1989, he was awarded the Nobel Prize for Peace for his efforts to end the Chinese rule of Tibet.

• Zen Buddhism

Zen Buddhism is another form of Mahayana Buddhism. It came from China, where it was called Ch'an, meaning meditation. Today, however, it is most popular in Japan. Zen teaches that everyone can achieve enlightenment, but not through the study of scriptures, worship or good deeds. Instead, Zen followers meditate for hours. They try to get beyond ordinary knowledge and reach sudden enlightenment. Some do so by thinking about riddles, called *koans*, which have no answer. One koan asks, "What is the sound of one hand clapping?"

The Spread of Buddhism

Although Buddhism began in India, it has fewer followers there than Hinduism does. Over the centuries, Buddhism has spread all over Asia and to Australia, Europe and the Americas. It has attracted many to its thoughtful way of life.

MARKING SPECIAL EVENTS

Joining the Community

There is no special ceremony when Buddhist children become adults, but there may be one when Buddhists join monasteries as monks and nuns. Their heads are shaved, and they give up all belongings except a robe and a begging bowl. They agree to follow the Five Precepts in their strictest form.

Weddings

Buddhists usually get married in a civil (non-religious) ceremony. But afterwards, the bride and groom may visit a temple or monastery to ask the monks for a blessing. Buddhist wedding rituals are more common in the West than in Asia.

Funerals

Funerals are important religious ceremonies for Buddhists. Usually, the dead body is cremated.

Tibetan Buddhists say that, after death, people do not immediately realize they are dead. During funerals, the monks say special verses, which they believe the dead can hear. After four days, the dead see a brilliant light. If they stay and face the light, they are freed from the cycle of rebirth. Most, however, run away and begin to seek a new life.

Each summer at full moon, people in Kandy, Sri Lanka, celebrate the Sacred Tooth of Buddha festival. Decorated elephants lead the parade.

FESTIVALS

Buddhist festivals vary in different countries. Many celebrate events in the life of the Buddha.

Wesak Day

The Buddha is said to have been born, reached enlightenment and died on the same day of the year. Theravada Buddhists call this day Wesak Day. At the full moon in April or May, they celebrate these events by decorating their houses, lighting candles to represent the Buddha's enlightenment, and giving gifts to monks. As an act of kindness, some people free captive birds to remember that the Buddha cared for all things.

Mahayana Buddhists celebrate the Buddha's birthday at the Flower Festival in spring.

To celebrate the Tibetan New Year, lamas chant and play long horns.

These North American Buddhist nuns meditate and live simple, compassionate lives.

SIKHISM

Compared to other major religions, Sikhism began recently — only five hundred years ago. It started in the Punjab area, which is now part of both India and Pakistan. The word "sikh" means disciple or student. Sikhs are followers of Guru Nanak, the religion's founder. In the two hundred years after Guru Nanak died, there were nine other gurus (teachers). The last, Guru Gobind Singh, declared that after he died, the Sikh sacred book should be treated as the guru. It became known as the Guru Granth Sahib.

As the religion grew, India's Mogul rulers tried to crush it. More recently, Sikhs have struggled against India's British rulers and later against the Hindu people, who are the majority in India. Many Sikhs have moved to other parts of the world, including North America.

THE LIFE OF GURU NANAK

Nanak was born into a Hindu family in 1469 C.E., a time when the Moguls (who were Muslims) ruled that part of the world. When Nanak grew up, he married and had two sons. Then, in his twenties, he left home and traveled. One of his companions was a Muslim musician, and another was a Hindu peasant.

QUICK FACTS

Followers: *25 million*

Locations: *Punjab area, United Kingdom, North America*

God: *one God*

Teacher/Founder: *Guru Nanak*

Scripture: *Guru Granth Sahib*

Places of worship: *gurdwaras*

Religious leaders: *granthi (any educated member)*

Major festivals: *Baisakhi, Guru Nanak's birthday*

Guru Nanak, founder of Sikhism

Nanak searched for a way to approach God directly. He came to believe that all people are equal — all castes, all religions and all men and women. His teachings attracted many followers, and he became known as a guru.

Eventually, Guru Nanak settled in a village called Kartarpur, or the City of the Creator. Before he died in 1539, he named another man as guru to succeed him. He did not choose his son, as many thought he would, but a man who had worked hard and served other people.

TEACHINGS AND BELIEFS

Guru Nanak taught that there is only one God, who created the universe and who is in everything. People can worship God directly, without rituals or priests. They can serve God by caring for each other, by living an honest life and by working hard. All people are equal, he said, and all can attain *mukti* (liberation). They are then one with God and free from the cycle of reincarnation, of endless deaths and rebirths.

SCRIPTURE

The central book of Sikhism is the Guru Granth Sahib. It contains hymns composed by Sikh gurus and by Hindu and Muslim poets. This book is kept in all Sikh temples. In homes, people place it in a room of its own.

WORSHIP

Sikhs worship anytime and anywhere by thinking about the hymns of the Guru Granth Sahib. However, they usually say prayers three times each day — in the morning, at sunset and before falling asleep.

The best-known Sikh holy site is the Golden Temple in Amritsar, a city in the Punjab. This square building sits in the center of a reflecting pool. The top two stories are plated in gold. The temple has a door on each of its four sides to represent its openness to people from the four corners of the earth.

The Gurdwara

The Sikh place of worship is called a *gurdwara*, or house of God. Many gurdwaras are large, but any building with a Guru Granth Sahib and a community kitchen and dining room can be a gurdwara. Gurdwaras also serve as places where people gather and learn.

Gurdwaras are open at all times to all people. Before entering, people remove their shoes and cover their heads in respect for the Guru Granth Sahib, which rests on cushions on a throne. They bow to the Guru Granth Sahib and make a donation of food or money, then back away. Men sit on one side and women on the other.

During the service, there are readings, singing and prayers led by a *granthi*, who can be any person who knows the scriptures. Afterwards, people get together in the dining room, where they sit on the floor and eat a simple vegetarian meal. All people, including outsiders, are welcome to join in the meal.

Sikhs prepare a meal in a gurdwara.

THE STORY OF THE KHALSA

The tenth guru, Gobind Singh, lived at a time when the Sikh religion and its followers were under attack from the Mogul emperors. Gobind Singh was a man of many talents — a poet, a skilled fighter and an archer. At a harvest festival in 1699, he gathered all the Sikhs together.

"Which of you is willing to offer his head for his religion?" he asked. At first no one moved; then one man stepped forward. Guru Gobind Singh took the man into a tent and later came out with a bloody sword. Again he asked the question.

Eventually, four more men offered to give up their heads for their religion. Each was taken into the tent, and each time the guru returned with a bloody sword. The horrified crowd believed that all had been killed.

Finally, Guru Gobind Singh brought out the five men, all dressed in splendid yellow clothes and each carrying a sword. The crowd gasped and cheered. Guru Gobind Singh named these five men the first members of the Khalsa, the pure Sikh community.

The first five members of the Khalsa were men who volunteered to die for their religion, but were rewarded instead.

To do away with caste distinctions, Guru Gobind Singh declared that Sikh men would take the name Singh, meaning lion, as a last or middle name. All women would take the name Kaur, meaning princess.

Khalsa Sikhs promise not to cut their hair, not to have sex outside marriage, and not to smoke, drink alcohol or take drugs. They eat the meat of only those animals that have been killed instantly with one stroke.

The Five Ks

Guru Gobind Singh introduced five symbols of the Sikh faith, called the Five Ks.
1. *Kesh* (hair) — Hair must not be cut.
2. *Kanga* (comb) — A comb must be carried in the hair to keep it neat.
3. *Kirpan* (sword) — A small sword is carried as a symbol of Sikhs' willingness to defend themselves and to fight against injustice. It is not to be used as a weapon.
4. *Kara* (bracelet) — Sikhs wear a steel bracelet. The circular shape represents the never-ending cycle of life, and the steel is a sign of strength.
5. *Kachha* (short pants) — These pants were once a part of the Sikh military uniform. They symbolize cleanliness and restraint.

At any special occasion or festival, the Guru Granth Sahib may be read all the way through. This reading takes about forty-eight hours.

MARKING SPECIAL EVENTS
Childhood

Shortly after a baby is born, Sikh parents visit the gurdwara to express their happiness and gratitude for the new family member. The Guru Granth Sahib is opened at random. The first letter of the hymn at the top left of the page becomes the first letter of the baby's name.

For Sikhs, the education of children is very important — especially learning the Punjabi language.

Weddings

Sikh families may take part in choosing marriage partners for their sons and daughters. At the wedding in the gurdwara, the bride and groom are taught their duties as husband and wife. They walk four times around the Guru Granth Sahib.

Traditionally, a Sikh bride wears a red salwar-kameez. The groom wears a pink or red turban.

Funerals

Sikhs do not feel that death is a time of terrible mourning, since death is part of all life. After a person dies, the body is washed and clothed, then cremated. The mourners recite the nighttime prayer. The ashes are usually placed in a river. No gravestones or monuments are allowed. Ten days later, more prayers and a reading of the Guru Granth Sahib bring an end to the period of mourning.

Amrit Ceremony

When Sikhs are ready, they are accepted into the Khalsa community in a ceremony called *amrit*. Five Khalsa members must be present. The person is told about the principles of Sikhism. Then water and sugar are stirred in a steel bowl using a two-edged sword. The person drinks this liquid five times. Afterwards, if the person does not already have a Sikh name, he or she is given one.

An amrit ceremony marks a Sikh's entry into the Khalsa community.

Sikh Clothes

In North America and Europe, many Sikhs wear Western clothes to work, but they change into traditional garments to go to the gurdwara. The men wear tight trousers and a long loose shirt, and the women wear a *salwar-kameez* (long pants and a tunic) or a sari. Women cover their heads with a long scarf.

Many Sikh men and some women wear a *turban*, which is a long piece of cotton fabric (about 5 m or 16 ft. long) that is wrapped around the head. Before they put on the turban, they put their hair in a bun and tie a cloth over it. Boys wear only a smaller cloth covering called a *patka* on their hair to keep it off their faces.

Some Sikh men combine traditional and Western clothing at work.

Guru Gobind Singh's birthday is a major Sikh festival. This girl wears a traditional costume to celebrate it.

FESTIVALS

Sikhs celebrate some of the same festivals as Hindus, including Diwali and Holi, although these have a different meaning for Sikhs. They also hold festivals to remember the births and deaths of the gurus. After a religious service at the gurdwara, people march in parades and give away food.

Baisakhi

The Baisakhi festival in April marks the anniversary of the founding of the Khalsa. All day there are prayers, readings and services at the gurdwara. People think about the spiritual path. Some prepare for the amrit ceremony when they will become members of the Khalsa. Then at night, after a communal meal, everyone gathers for songs and dances.

Two colorful dances — the Bhangra and the Giddha — are part of the Baisakhi festival.

JAINISM

The followers of Jainism, called Jains, do not believe in a God or a creator. Instead they follow the example of Tirthankaras (pronounced tir-TEN-keras), perfect human teachers who, they believe, lived in the distant past.

Mahavira, also known as Vardhamana or the Great Hero, founded the religion. Jains believe that he was the last of the twenty-four Tirthankaras. Mahavira lived in India in the sixth century B.C.E., at about the same time and place as the Buddha. He gave up his comfortable life and lived for twelve years as a beggar. After that, he attained enlightenment.

TEACHINGS AND BELIEFS

Jainism grew out of Hinduism and shares many beliefs with the older religion.

The idea of *ahimsa*, which means non-injury, is even more important to Jains than to Hindus. Jains care for all animals and try never to kill them — even insects. The Jain belief in non-violence was very important in the life of Mahatma Gandhi, who was a Hindu.

Jains also give up things that are pleasurable in order to be freed from karma. They see karma as actions that keep the soul stuck in a cycle of reincarnation. Some Jains become monks and nuns and give up even more things. Many cover their mouths to avoid breathing in any insects by mistake. One group of monks gives up all clothing and walks about naked.

Jains believe that they must follow the Three Jewels: right knowledge, faith and actions. Their belief in non-violence determines what jobs they may and may not hold. For example, Jains may be merchants or lawyers, but they cannot become butchers. Jainism also encourages its followers to give to the poor.

FESTIVAL

Paryusana

The festival of Paryusana lasts for eight or ten days during August or September. It is a serious occasion that encourages respect for all life. Some Jains live as monks or nuns for a few days. During the ceremonies, people read from the Kalpa Sutra, their sacred book. On the last day, they fast, give money to the poor and ask forgiveness from anyone they have hurt.

QUICK FACTS

Followers: *4 million*

Location: *India*

Teacher/Founder: *Mahavira*

Scripture: *Kalpa Sutra*

Places of worship: *temples and meditation halls*

Religious leaders: *monks and nuns*

Major festival: *Paryusana*

A Jain monk covers his mouth to avoid harming insects.

JUDAISM

Judaism (pronounced JOO-dee-ism) is the religion of the Jewish people. Judaism traces its beginnings to one man, Abraham, who lived about four thousand years ago in the Middle East. According to the Hebrew Bible,

God made an agreement, called a *covenant*, with Abraham. God promised to take care of Abraham and his people forever, if they would obey God's laws.

Judaism is a *monotheistic* religion. This means that Jews believe there is only one God.

THE STORY OF THE PROMISED LAND

The story of the Jewish people is told in the Hebrew Bible, so called because it was written in the Hebrew language.

When Abraham was an old man, the story says, God spoke to him and told him to take his family to Canaan (now Israel). God promised Abraham that he would become the

father of a great nation. In Canaan, Abraham and his wife, Sarah, had a son, Isaac. After Abraham died, food became hard to find, so Isaac's son Jacob left the Promised Land and took his family to Egypt.

Jacob, whom God named Israel, had twelve sons. For a time, his sons and their families, called the Israelites, did well in Egypt. But about 1300 B.C.E., a pharaoh who ruled Egypt made slaves of the Israelites. He also ordered that all the Israelite boys should be killed at birth. One mother hid her baby and placed him in a small basket on the River Nile. He was later found by the pharaoh's daughter, who named him Moses and raised him.

Moses Leads His People

One day, when Moses had grown up, he saw an Egyptian boss beating an Israelite. In anger, Moses killed the Egyptian and ran away. The Hebrew Bible says that God then spoke to Moses and told him to take his people back to Canaan. Moses returned to Egypt and asked the pharaoh to let his people go, but the pharaoh refused.

In the story, God punished Egypt by sending ten terrible plagues, including lice and locusts. The last plague killed all the eldest sons in the land. But because the Israelites had marked their doorways, their children were left alone or "passed over." This night is celebrated every year at the holiday of Passover.

QUICK FACTS

Followers: *14.7 million*

Locations: *Israel, Russia, Europe, North America and elsewhere*

Major branches: *Orthodox, Conservative, Reform*

God: *one God*

Teachers/Founders: *Abraham, Moses*

Scriptures: *Hebrew Bible, Talmud*

Places of worship: *synagogues, temples*

Religious leaders: *rabbis*

Major festivals: *Rosh Hashanah (New Year), Yom Kippur (Day of Atonement), Passover*

The Red Sea parts, allowing Moses to lead the Israelites out of Egypt.

That final plague convinced the pharaoh to let the Israelites leave Egypt. But later he changed his mind and sent his armies to chase after them. God divided the waters of the Red (or Reed) Sea so that Moses and his people could escape. Then the waters closed over the Egyptian soldiers.

After many hardships in the desert, the Israelites arrived at Mount Sinai. On the mountaintop, God gave Moses stone tablets on which were written the Ten Commandments. These were the rules that God wanted the Israelites to follow. Years later, the people reached Canaan, the Promised Land. But Moses died before he could enter it.

King David

In the centuries that followed, the Israelites were ruled by kings. The greatest was King David, who, as a young man, fought against his enemy's champion, Goliath. David's son Solomon built a temple in Jerusalem. The temple was destroyed twice — once in 586 B.C.E. when the Babylonians forced the Jewish people into exile, and again in 70 C.E. when the Romans conquered them.

In Jerusalem, Jews pray at the Western Wall, a surviving part of the temple destroyed by the Romans.

This seven-branched candleholder, or menorah, is a symbol of the Jewish people.

The Holocaust

At many times in their history, Jews have been badly treated by those in power. During the Holocaust of the 1940s, the Nazi government of Germany ordered the killing of six million Jews.

Israel

The name "Israel" has many meanings. Isaac's son Jacob was renamed Israel. The group or nation that Abraham founded is also called Israel. In 1948, modern Israel was founded as a Jewish state, and many Jews moved there from other countries. Today, about one-third of all Jewish people live in Israel.

The six-pointed Star of David appears on the Israeli flag.

The Ten Commandments

1. I am the Lord your God. You will have no other Gods besides me.
2. Do not make any images of God.
3. Do not swear or curse using God's name.
4. Remember the Sabbath day and keep it holy.
5. Honor your father and mother.
6. Do not commit murder.
7. Do not cheat on your marriage partner.
8. Do not steal.
9. Do not tell lies about other people in court.
10. Do not desire things that belong to other people.

TEACHINGS AND BELIEFS

Jews believe in one God who created the universe and everything in it. They believe that God spoke to Abraham and Moses. God promised to care for their people and gave them rules to follow. The most important rules are the Ten Commandments, which are also followed by Christians.

SCRIPTURES

All Jews are expected to study the Hebrew Bible, which has three main parts: the Torah, the Prophets and the Writings.

The Torah

The Torah, also called the Five Books of Moses, begins with the story of creation — how God created the universe in six days and rested on the seventh. It goes on to tell the stories of Adam and Eve, of Noah and the Flood, of Abraham and of Moses. As well as the stories and the Ten Commandments, the Torah gives rules for daily life and for worship.

The Prophets and the Writings

The Prophets tell more about Jewish history and God's moral teachings. The Psalms — poems or hymns — are a well-known part of the Writings. One psalm begins, "The Lord is my shepherd, I shall not want." Other psalms praise God, give thanks and express great joy.

The Midrash and the Talmud

Many Jewish scholars have discussed the meaning of the Hebrew Bible and how it applies to life. Their comments are gathered into many books, including the Midrash and the Talmud, as a record of the oral tradition.

The Shema

The Shema is a prayer that forms an important part of religious services. It begins:

"Hear, O Israel: The Lord is our God, the Lord is One. And thou shalt love the Lord thy God with all thy heart, with all thy soul and with all thy might. And these words, which I command thee this day, shall be upon thy heart; and thou shalt teach them diligently unto thy children."

Mezuzah

A small box is nailed on the doorframes of many Jewish houses. This mezuzah contains a scroll with important words from the Hebrew Bible on it. Some people kiss their fingers and then touch the mezuzah as they enter the house.

A rabbi uses a pointer called a yad to read the Torah.

WORSHIP

Jews worship in a building called a *synagogue* (pronounced SIN-a-gog). Every synagogue contains the Torah. Handwritten on parchment and rolled into scrolls, the Torah is kept in a cabinet called the Ark.

Religious Jews pray three times a day — on waking, in the afternoon and in the evening. In addition, they may gather with others for weekly or daily services at the synagogue. Ten adult Jews, a *minyan*, must be present for services to take place. The services may be led by a *rabbi* (religious teacher), by a *cantor* (leader of singing), or by any adult member of the synagogue.

The most important services are held on the Sabbath, the day on which the people rest, as God rested on the seventh day of creation. The Sabbath begins at sunset on Friday evening and lasts until sunset on Saturday.

On Friday nights, families get together. They wear their best clothes and eat a meal that was prepared earlier, since no cooking or

This man wears a tallit (shawl) and tefillin (small boxes).

other work is allowed on the Sabbath. Family members light candles and say a blessing. It is a time to enjoy together. Services are held at the synagogue on Friday night and on Saturday.

Garments for Prayer

To remind themselves of God's commandments and to follow the instructions of the Torah, Jews wear three garments during prayers:

The *tallit* is a shawl with fringes at the corners.

The *tefillin* are two small leather boxes containing words from the Torah. One is tied to the forehead and the other to the left, or weaker, arm.

A small hat called a *yarmulke* (pronounced YA-mick-a) is worn in synagogue and sometimes for other occasions as well. Some married Orthodox Jewish women wear a wig or hat to cover their heads in public.

In a Reform synagogue, a woman rabbi approaches the Ark.

FOOD RULES

The Hebrew Bible contains rules about which foods Jewish people may and may not eat. The foods that may be eaten are called *kosher*. These include fish that have scales and fins (not shellfish), birds that eat grain (chickens, but not birds of prey), mammals that have split hooves and that chew their cud (cows, but not pigs), edible plants, milk and eggs.

Animals intended for food must be killed in a humane way that drains their blood. Blessings are said before their lives are taken.

At a kosher meal, meat and milk may not be eaten together. Jewish families often have two sets of dishes — one for meat and one for dairy. They may also keep another set just for Passover.

MARKING SPECIAL EVENTS
Childhood

Eight days after birth, Jewish boys are circumcised. This removal of the foreskin of the penis is a mark of the covenant between God and the Jews. At this ceremony, the boy is also given his Hebrew name, which may be different from the one he uses every day. Girl babies are often blessed and named at the synagogue.

Bar Mitzvah

At age thirteen, boys are welcomed into the congregation at a ceremony called a *bar mitzvah* ("bar" means son and "mitzvah" means commandment). Afterwards, the boys may take part in religious services and be counted as part of the minyan, the ten people needed for services in a synagogue.

The ceremony for girls is called a *bat mitzvah* ("bat" means daughter). In Reform and some Conservative congregations, girls may then become part of the minyan.

In preparation for his bar mitzvah, a boy learns a passage from the Torah.

Standing under a canopy, a bride and groom share a glass of wine.

Weddings

Weddings bless the bride and groom and mark the beginning of a new family. Ceremonies may be held at a synagogue or elsewhere. The bride and groom stand under a canopy that represents their new home and make a promise to love and care for each other. They share a glass of wine. At the end, the groom breaks a glass with his foot to remember the destruction of the Temple in Jerusalem.

Funerals

After a person dies, the body is washed and wrapped in white cloth, then buried as soon as possible. Cremation is not allowed. One week of mourning, called *shiva*, follows. During this time, close relatives stay at home and do no work. To comfort and help the family, friends visit and bring food. For eleven months after death, family members say a special prayer every day. Afterwards, prayers are repeated once a year.

Branches of Judaism

In the past few centuries, different groups have formed among Jews.

Orthodox Jews believe that the Torah came directly from God, and they follow traditional Jewish law closely.

Conservative and Reform Jews believe that Jewish tradition can sometimes be changed to suit changing times.

Some Jews do not practice the rituals of religion, but they do feel that they belong to a group with its own culture and history.

FESTIVALS

Many Jewish festivals help Jewish people remember their history. Others remind them of the spiritual side of life.

A ram's horn is blown on Rosh Hashanah.

Rosh Hashanah and Yom Kippur

Two especially holy times occur in the early fall. Rosh Hashanah is the Jewish New Year. It begins a period of ten days during which people think about their deeds in the past year. Then on Yom Kippur, the Day of Atonement, they ask for forgiveness. Jews do not work or eat on this very solemn day.

Hanukkah

Hanukkah, a favorite holiday for children, falls in December. It commemorates a time about two thousand years ago when a group of Jews fought and won a battle for the freedom to practice their religion. To celebrate, they gathered in the Temple in Jerusalem. There was only a little oil left in the lamp, but miraculously it burned for eight days. To remember this time, family members light candles on a *menorah* (candleholder) with nine branches. Eight of the candles represent the eight days. The ninth candle is used to light the others.

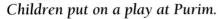

Children put on a play at Purim.

Purim

Another holiday children love is Purim. This happy festival celebrates the cleverness and bravery of Queen Esther, who saved the Jewish people from Haman, a man who was trying to destroy them.

Passover

In the spring, Passover reminds Jews of the time that the Israelite children were saved from death before their escape from Egypt. On the first night of Passover, they place special foods on the dinner table. One is a flatbread called *matzo* (pronounced MOT-soh), used because the Israelites had no time to let bread rise before they had to escape. In addition, there are bitter herbs for the suffering of the Israelites, an egg for new life, a fruit and nut mixture for the mortar they used to build the pyramids, and wine for the joy they felt at their escape.

The youngest child at the table asks four questions about why this night is different from other nights. The answers tell the story of Passover.

CHRISTIANITY

Children all over the world look forward to Christmas every year. It celebrates the birth of Jesus, a man who preached in the Middle East about two thousand years ago. Since then, the teachings of Jesus have spread over most of the world. Now, about one-third of the people on earth are Christian.

Jesus is called the Christ, meaning the one chosen by God. Christians believe that Jesus is the Messiah who was promised to the Jewish people in the Hebrew Bible.

Christianity, like Judaism, is a *monotheistic* (meaning one God) religion. And like the Jews, Christians trace their ancestors back to Abraham.

THE LIFE OF JESUS

The story of Jesus' life is told in the New Testament, the second part of the Christian Bible.

Jesus was born into a Jewish family. His mother was named Mary, and his father, Joseph, was a carpenter. Jesus grew up in Nazareth (in present-day Israel), which was then ruled by Rome. As a child, he learned about Judaism.

When he was thirty, Jesus met John the Baptist, a prophet who told people to expect the Messiah soon. John baptized Jesus and many other people in the River Jordan. Soon

Mary holds her baby, Jesus.

afterward, Jesus began traveling from place to place, teaching and telling *parables* (stories with a message). He told people about his Father in heaven, and he taught that God was a God of love.

The Bible says that Jesus healed people and performed miracles, such as walking on water and feeding many people from just a little bread and a few fish. Among the many people who followed him were twelve men, called his disciples or apostles.

Not everyone was pleased with what Jesus said. The Roman rulers worried that he was encouraging people to revolt, and some Jewish leaders thought he was telling his followers to break religious rules.

Jesus feeds a crowd with just a few fish and loaves of bread.

In this mosaic, Jesus is shown with a halo as a sign of his holiness.

The Last Supper

When he was about thirty-three, Jesus visited Jerusalem at the time of Passover. He ate the Passover meal with his twelve disciples. Before the meal, Judas, one of the twelve, had agreed to betray Jesus to the high priest and council. Jesus was arrested and tried. Pilate, the Roman ruler, condemned him to death by crucifixion. After Jesus died, his friends buried his body in a cave.

Crucifixion was a common but terrible form of execution. The person was nailed or tied to a wooden cross and left to die.

According to Christian beliefs, miraculous events followed. Three days later, on a Sunday, some women followers went to the cave and found it empty. Over the next forty days, many people said they had seen Jesus. They believed he had risen from death. This miracle is called the Resurrection.

After Jesus died, some of his followers wrote down what they had seen and what they had heard him say. These writings became the books of Matthew, Mark, Luke and John in the Christian Bible.

Paul became a Christian after he had a vision of Jesus.

THE SPREAD OF CHRISTIANITY

After Jesus' death, his apostles talked to people about his teachings. They said that Jesus had risen from death and was the promised Messiah. Groups of believers began to meet together and set up new churches.

Paul, who was a Jew and a Roman citizen, persecuted these early Christians. Then, on the road to Damascus, Paul had a vision of Jesus and became a Christian himself. Paul thought that the new religion should not be limited to Jews. Therefore, he traveled to many cities in the Roman Empire, spreading the word about Jesus. His letters to new churches helped to put Christian beliefs into words.

At first, the Roman rulers tried to stop Christianity. They arrested many Christians, including Paul. After three hundred years, however, Emperor Constantine decided to make Christianity the official religion of the Roman Empire.

QUICK FACTS

Followers: *2.3 billion*

Locations: *Europe, North America, South America, Australia, Russia, southern Africa, parts of Asia*

Major branches: *Roman Catholic, Eastern Orthodox, Protestant*

God: *one God*

Teacher/Founder: *Jesus*

Scripture: *Bible (Old Testament and New Testament)*

Places of worship: *churches, chapels, cathedrals*

Religious leaders: *priests, ministers*

Major festivals: *Easter, Christmas*

A children's choir sings at a Christian church service.

Old Testament

The first part of the Christian Bible contains the Hebrew Bible, which most Christians call the Old Testament. It tells the story of God's part in the history of the Jews, and mentions the coming of a Messiah, who, Christians believe, was Jesus.

New Testament

The second part of the Christian Bible, called the New Testament, was written after Jesus died. The first four books — Matthew, Mark, Luke and John — are called the Gospels (meaning good news). Each one tells the story of Jesus' life, teachings, death and resurrection.

The next book, Acts of the Apostles, talks about the early history of the religion and about the people, especially Paul, who spread Jesus' teachings.

Next come the Epistles, which are letters by Paul and others to Christians around the Mediterranean Sea.

The last book, Revelation, describes the end of time, when Jesus is expected to return. At this time, the souls of the dead will be judged.

TEACHINGS AND BELIEFS

Christians believe in one God who created the universe. For Christians, God includes the Father, the Son (Jesus), and the Holy Spirit. Together these three are called the Holy Trinity.

According to Christian belief, Jesus was both human and divine. As the son of God, he was sent to earth to save human beings from sin and death. As the child of a human mother, Mary, he suffered pain and died on the cross.

Jesus taught people to love and care for each other and to forgive their enemies. He promised God would forgive them and give them eternal life. Jesus said that the greatest commandment was to love God with your whole heart and mind and to love your neighbor as yourself.

The cross — this one is Celtic — is a symbol of Christianity.

The Apostles' Creed

Over the centuries, religious leaders tried to define clearly what it meant to be Christian. They wrote creeds, statements of what they believed (*credo* means "I believe" in Latin). The Apostles' Creed is one example, written about 400 C.E.

"I believe in God, the Father Almighty, creator of heaven and earth. I believe in Jesus Christ, his only Son, our Lord. He was conceived by the power of the Holy Spirit and born of the Virgin Mary. He suffered under Pontius Pilate, was crucified, died, and was buried. He descended to the dead. On the third day he rose again. He ascended into heaven and is seated at the right hand of the Father. He will come again to judge the living and the dead. I believe in the Holy Spirit, the holy catholic [universal] Church, the communion of saints, the forgiveness of sins, the resurrection of the body, and the life everlasting. Amen."

WORSHIP

Sunday, the day that Jesus rose from the dead, is the day Christians gather in buildings called churches for worship. Services usually include Bible readings and prayer. Prayers can praise or thank God. They can also ask for forgiveness or for help. The congregation often says the Lord's Prayer together. In addition, the people may sing hymns, and a member of the clergy may give a sermon.

Some churches are huge and highly decorated, while others are plain and simple. Some services are attended by hundreds of people and include a choir, organ music and special robes for the clergy. Other services are quiet, even silent, with only a few people present.

At the Passover meal that Jesus ate with his disciples before his death (called the Last Supper), he told his followers to eat bread and drink wine

The Lord's Prayer

Jesus taught his followers to say the Lord's Prayer (found in Matthew 6: 9–13):

"Our Father, who art in heaven, hallowed be thy Name. Thy kingdom come. Thy will be done, on earth as it is in heaven. Give us this day our daily bread. And forgive us our trespasses, as we forgive those who trespass against us. And lead us not into temptation, but deliver us from evil."

Many Protestants add: "For thine is the kingdom, the power and the glory, forever and ever, Amen."

to remember him. At many church services, those gathered take part in Communion, also called the Mass or the Eucharist. The people eat bread or a wafer and drink wine or juice, as Jesus instructed. The bread and wine symbolize the body and blood of Christ.

Christians also pray at home, especially before meals and at bedtime.

In this stained window, a mother brings her child to speak with Jesus.

The Last Supper was a Passover meal that Jesus shared with his twelve disciples.

BRANCHES OF CHRISTIANITY

Over the centuries, disagreements led groups of Christians to form separate branches. The first major split took place one thousand years ago, when early Christians divided into the Roman Catholic Church and the Eastern Orthodox Church.

Another division took place in the 1500s. Martin Luther, a German priest, protested against what he saw as abuses in the Roman Catholic Church. This led to the Reformation, when people who agreed with Luther — called Protestants — separated from the Roman church.

Also in the 1500s, King Henry VIII of England broke away from the Roman Catholic Church and set himself up as the head of the Church of England. This branch is also known as the Anglican Church.

Roman Catholic

The Roman Catholic Church is headed by the Pope, who lives in the Vatican in Rome, Italy. Under the Pope are archbishops, bishops and priests.

The Pope is the head of the Roman Catholic Church.

Tourists throng the square outside St. Mark's Basilica in Venice, Italy. Built 1000 years ago, the cathedral is richly decorated with mosaics and gold.

These religious leaders are all men and may not marry. Priests offer the Mass and administer the seven sacraments. During the Middle Ages, magnificent large churches — called cathedrals — were built all over Europe. Inside most cathedrals and smaller churches are paintings or statues of Jesus and of Mary, his mother.

Eastern Orthodox

The first center for the Eastern Orthodox Church was Constantinople (now Istanbul) in Turkey. Today there are Eastern Orthodox Churches in many countries including Greece, Russia, Serbia and Ukraine. Each of these Churches is headed by a bishop, although the patriarch of Constantinople is seen as their leader. Eastern Orthodox cathedrals are often colorful buildings with onion-shaped domes on top.

A Russian Orthodox patriarch stands in front of a cathedral.

Protestant

There are many different Protestant Churches, called denominations. They include Lutherans, Baptists, Episcopalians, Presbyterians, Methodists, Pentecostals and many others. In most denominations, each local church is independent and hires its own minister. Ministers may be men or women, single or married. Protestants stress the importance of reading and understanding the Bible. Church services include readings from the Bible, the singing of hymns, and the preaching of a sermon by the minister.

A simple wooden church braves the ocean winds in Trinity, Newfoundland, Canada — a town settled by men and women who fished for cod.

An Anglican priest conducts a church service.

The Anglican Church has spread around the world. Its head is the Archbishop of Canterbury in England. Anglican church services are full of music, and they sometimes use incense, as do the Roman Catholics. Anglican priests and bishops are allowed to marry, and in some countries women can be

In most churches, the people sit in pews facing the altar or communion table.

◆ PROFILE ◆

MOTHER TERESA

Christian nuns and monks lead lives of contemplation and prayer, but they also work with people in need.

Mother Teresa was a Roman Catholic nun who moved from Yugoslavia to India. Joined by a group of dedicated nuns, she spent fifty years caring for poor children and dying people in Calcutta and elsewhere. She inspired people around the world to offer their help and was awarded the Nobel Peace Prize in 1979.

MARKING SPECIAL EVENTS

Christians mark the stages of life with rituals called *sacraments*. Some Churches include only a few sacraments, others up to seven. Two — baptism and communion — are common to most.

Baptism

Baptism, or christening, usually takes place soon after birth. At this time, the child begins life as part of the Christian community. Just as John the Baptist baptized Jesus in water, priests and ministers baptize babies by dipping them into water or sprinkling water on their foreheads. Adults may also be baptized into the Christian religion.

A Protestant minister baptizes a baby.

Confirmation

Confirmation may take place when the infant is baptized (Eastern Orthodox) or some years later (Roman Catholic and Protestant). After studying the religion, children, teenagers or adults are confirmed in their commitment to Christianity in a special ceremony.

Communion

Communion (the Mass or the Eucharist) is a ritual that recalls the Last Supper, which Jesus shared with his disciples. It may be celebrated in churches during regular services, or in homes or hospitals for the sick.

A bride and groom exchange rings.

Weddings

Marriages usually take place in church. The bride often wears a long white dress and carries flowers. The bride and groom promise to love and care for each other for life. The bride, and sometimes the groom as well, receives a gold ring to wear on the fourth finger of the left hand.

Funerals

Christians believe in a life after death. After someone dies, a funeral is held to comfort family and friends and to pass the person on to the care of God. Burial or cremation follows.

Catholic children receive their first Communion.

FESTIVALS

The festivals and holidays of the Christian calendar mark events in the life of Jesus.

Christmas

At Christmas, people celebrate Jesus' birth. No one knows his exact birth date, but Christians have chosen December 25 as the date. (Eastern Orthodox Christians celebrate the arrival of the wise men — Epiphany — on January 6.)

The season begins with Advent, four Sundays before Christmas. This is a time of preparation. Children often receive special calendars with windows to open each day until Christmas day.

At Christmas time, children hang bright decorations on an evergreen tree.

This Central American nativity scene includes figures of Mary, Joseph and baby Jesus.

The Christmas Story

The Gospels tell the Christmas story. It begins with Joseph and Mary's trip to Bethlehem to pay taxes, before Jesus was born. Mary and Joseph could find nowhere to stay, so they took shelter in a stable. After Jesus was born, his mother laid him in a manger, a place where animals are fed.

That night, shepherds heard angels singing, telling them of Jesus' birth. They rushed to Bethlehem to see the child. Twelve days later, wise men, who had followed a bright star to the stable, presented gifts to the baby Jesus.

For children, Easter eggs are a favorite tradition. These decorated eggs represent new life, as a chick hatches from an egg.

Easter

The most important time in the Christian year is the Easter season, the time that Jesus traveled to Jerusalem, died and was resurrected. Easter occurs on a different date each year, between mid-March and late April. (The date on which Western Christians celebrate Easter is the first Sunday after the first full moon after March 21.)

The forty weekdays before Easter are called Lent. During this time, children and adults often give up something they enjoy, such as dessert. Lent is a time for prayers and serious thought.

The week before Easter Sunday is called Holy Week. The Sunday before Easter, Palm Sunday, recalls Jesus' entry into Jerusalem. Maundy Thursday recalls the Last Supper, and Good Friday is the day Jesus was crucified. Easter Sunday is a time of joyful celebration. On that day, Jesus' followers found that he had risen from the dead.

ISLAM

One spot in the world is central to Muslims, the followers of Islam. That place is Mecca, on the Arabian peninsula. Five times a day, all over the world, Muslims stop what they are doing, face toward Mecca and pray. At least once in their lives, Muslims try to make a trip to Mecca.

Islam is a *monotheistic* (meaning one God) religion. Like Judaism and Christianity, it began in the Middle East and traces its beginnings back to Abraham. The name "Islam" means submission or obedience to God and comes from a word meaning peace.

Islam is based on the Qur'an and teachings of the Prophet Muhammad, who lived about 1400 years ago. He taught that there is only one God, who is all-powerful. Islam's teachings also cover politics, art, science, family life, financial matters and social issues.

THE LIFE OF MUHAMMAD

Muhammad was born about 570 C.E. in Mecca, in what is now the country of Saudi Arabia. Many caravans of trade goods traveled through the city. Mecca also had a temple called the Ka'ba, containing many idols as well as a black stone.

Muhammad's father died before he was born, and his mother died

La Mezquita, an ancient mosque in Cordoba, Spain, was founded in the eighth century. Over 800 columns topped with red-and-white arches fill the space where thousands of worshipers came to pray.

shortly after his birth. His grandfather and his uncle raised him. As an adult, he went to work for a wealthy widow, Khadija, whom he later married. Muhammad was troubled by the fighting he saw around him. He was also upset when he saw that people were worshiping idols in the Ka'ba. He often went off by himself to meditate.

Once, when Muhammad was about forty, he was meditating in a cave. He saw a vision of the angel Gabriel, who told him that he had been selected by God to be a prophet. "Recite," the angel ordered three times. "What shall I recite?" asked Muhammad. In answer, the angel gave him a message from God, and Muhammad memorized the words.

QUICK FACTS

Followers: *1.5 billion*

Locations: *Middle East, North and West Africa, southeastern Europe, Central Asia, Pakistan, India, Bangladesh, Malaysia, Indonesia and elsewhere*

Major branches: *Sunni, Shi'ite*

God: *one God (Allah)*

Teacher/Prophet: *Muhammad*

Scripture: *Qur'an (also spelled Koran)*

Places of worship: *mosques*

Religious leaders: *imams*

Major festivals: *Festival of Fast Breaking, Festival of Sacrifice*

On a pilgrimage to Mecca, Muslims circle the Ka'ba seven times.

Preaching God's Message

Muhammad continued to receive these messages. He soon began preaching about God's power and goodness. He also criticized Mecca's people for worshiping idols. Some people liked his teachings, but others persecuted him and his companions. Eventually, in 622 C.E., he was forced to flee from Mecca to Medina, a city a short distance to the north. This flight, called the *Hijra*, marks the first year of the Islamic calendar.

In Medina, Muhammad invited people, including Christians and Jews, to become Muslims. He gradually became a powerful leader with a growing Islamic empire. By 630, he ruled most of the Arabian peninsula, including Mecca. When he returned to Mecca, he ordered that all the idols be removed from the Ka'ba and then he walked around the building seven times.

From a tall tower called a minaret, a man calls Muslims to prayer. He cries out: "Allah is most great. I testify that Muhammad is the prophet of Allah. Come to prayer. Come to salvation. Allah is most great. There is no God but Allah."

THE SPREAD OF ISLAM

By the time Muhammad died in 632, he had not chosen anyone to take on his role as leader. Over the next hundred years, his successors, called *caliphs*, continued to expand his empire. Eventually, it reached from Spain in the west to India in the east. Today, some countries have Islamic governments.

BRANCHES OF ISLAM

There are two main groups of Muslims, the Sunnis and the Shi'ites (pronounced SHE-ites). After Muhammad died, he was succeeded by three caliphs who were companions of Muhammad. They were accepted by the Sunnis, who make up 85 percent of all Muslims.

The fourth caliph was Ali, Muhammad's son-in-law. Shi'ites believe that Ali and his descendants are Muhammad's only true successors. They also give greater power to *imams*, or religious leaders. Shi'ites live mainly in Iran and Iraq.

TEACHINGS AND BELIEFS

The basic beliefs of Islam are summed up in this statement of faith: "I believe in Allah, his angels, his books and prophets and the Day of Judgment."

- "Allah" is the Arabic name for God, the all-powerful and merciful creator of all things.
- Angels are invisible and obey the commands of Allah. The angel Gabriel brought Allah's message to Muhammad and the other prophets.
- The Muslim holy book is the Qur'an (pronounced kur-AN).
- The prophets of Islam include Adam, Abraham, Noah, Moses and Jesus.
- On the Day of Judgment, those who have been good will be rewarded with Paradise, and those who have been evil will be sent to hell.

These are many of the names of Allah, including the Lord of the Universe, the All-Wise.

The Five Pillars of Islam

1. Faith — Muslims recite a statement of faith called the Shahada: "There is no God but Allah, and Muhammad is the Messenger of Allah."
2. Prayer — Muslims pray five times a day — before dawn, at noon, in mid-afternoon, at dusk and after dark. They can pray in a *mosque* (the Muslim place of worship) or in any clean place. A mat, or prayer rug, is sometimes placed on the floor. The person washes his or her face, arms and feet, then prays facing the Ka'ba in Mecca. Some Muslims carry a compass to help them locate the right direction. The prayers are said in Arabic, although Muslims can make special requests to God in their own language.
3. Almsgiving — Muslims give a portion of their money to care for the poor.
4. Fasting — Muslims fast during Ramadan, the month in which the angel first appeared to Muhammad. Muslims do not eat or drink from dawn to dusk each day of that month.
5. Pilgrimage — Everyone who is able goes on a pilgrimage, or Hajj, at least once in his or her lifetime. Pilgrims travel to the city of Mecca, where they put on simple clothes, so that everyone is equal, and circle the Ka'ba seven times. At the end of the pilgrimage they celebrate the Festival of Sacrifice, Eid ul-Adha.

SCRIPTURES

The holy book of Islam is the Qur'an. Muslims believe it is the word of God as recited by the angel Gabriel to Muhammad. Muhammad memorized God's messages immediately and taught them to his companions, who also memorized them. Scribes wrote down the words after they checked their accuracy with Muhammad.

The Qur'an has 114 chapters, which include instructions on spiritual, moral, social and legal matters; comments on people in the Bible; and descriptions of heaven and hell.

Other important books contain the deeds and sayings of the Prophet Muhammad. These help Muslims to understand the Qur'an.

LAW AND DAILY LIFE

Islam has many laws that tell people how to behave in their daily lives. Religion is part of family life, society, business and politics.

Islamic law forbids drinking alcohol, gambling, making or worshiping idols, charging interest on loans and saying bad things about other people.

Many Muslim women wear a veil covering all or part of their faces.

Muslims are not allowed to eat the meat of pigs. Animals must be killed in a way that causes the least pain and that drains the blood. Foods that Muslims are permitted to eat are called *halal*.

Jihad

The word "jihad" (pronounced jih-HOD) means striving to do things in God's way. Muslims may struggle against their own bad thoughts or actions. They may also struggle — using thoughts, words or deeds — against those who attack them. Islam teaches that violence should be used only as a defence.

Dervishes of the Sufi branch of Islam whirl and dance in praise of Allah.

These Muslim men are praying in a large mosque. Women pray in a separate area.

WORSHIP

A mosque can be small, but it is often a large building with an open courtyard and an inner space for prayer. Beautiful writing and intricate patterns may decorate the walls, but no pictures of humans or animals are allowed inside the mosque. The wall that is closest to the Ka'ba contains an alcove called a *mihrab*. From here, the imam leads prayer. On the same wall is a pulpit that he uses for delivering a sermon. The imam is chosen by the people for his knowledge and wisdom.

Muslims can pray almost anywhere — in a school, a field, a factory — but it is better to pray in a mosque. They remove their shoes before entering the mosque and wash their face, arms and feet. Women may attend in a special area. The worshipers form rows on the carpeted floor, facing Mecca. They say prayers in a series of positions — standing, bowing and kneeling with the head touching the floor.

Friday is a special day for Muslims. It is not a day of rest, but in Muslim countries all work stops around noon for services. On Fridays, the services are longer, and the imam preaches a sermon.

The mihrab (prayer alcove) indicates the direction of the Ka'ba.

MARKING SPECIAL EVENTS
Childhood

At birth or soon after, a father whispers the call to prayer in a baby's ear so that it is the first thing the baby hears. The child is named seven days later, when the family gathers and offers a sacrifice. Boys are circumcised.

Muslim children are taught the Arabic language and learn prayers and parts of the Qur'an by heart. In some parts of the world, families celebrate when a child first reads from the Qur'an, at about age four. Until age thirteen or so, children are encouraged but not required to take part in religious duties.

These girls are learning Arabic, so they can read the Qu'ran.

Muslim weddings may take place at home or at a mosque.

Weddings

All Muslims are encouraged to marry. Marriage is both a legal agreement and a religious covenant. Weddings are often arranged with the help of families. The ceremony is quite brief and can take place anywhere. No religious leader needs to be present — the couple simply state before witnesses that they are willing to marry.

Funerals

After death, the body is washed and wrapped in a white cloth. Prayers are said before the body is buried facing Mecca.

FESTIVALS

There are two main festivals, or *eids*, in the Islamic year. Because the Muslim calendar is based on the moon, festivals fall on different dates every year.

The Festival of Fast Breaking

The Festival of Fast Breaking, or Eid ul-Fitr, occurs at the end of Ramadan, the month when adults fast from dawn to dusk. Children may fast for short periods, which get longer as they grow up. Fasting teaches self-discipline and helps people understand and care for others.

Ramadan ends when the new moon can be seen, an event that is signaled to Muslims around the world. On this happy day, Eid ul-Fitr, families visit each other and exchange gifts and food. Prayers are said, and food is given to the poor.

Eid ul-Fitr is a joyful celebration marking the end of Ramadan.

The Festival of Sacrifice

The Festival of Sacrifice, Eid ul-Adha, occurs at the end of the pilgrimage to Mecca. People who have gone to Mecca celebrate there, while others celebrate at home. Eid ul-Adha recalls the time when Abraham was told by God to sacrifice his son Ishmael. When Abraham proved his obedience to God by tying his son to the altar, God allowed him to sacrifice a sheep instead.

ZOROASTRIANISM

 Zoroastrianism was founded by the Persian prophet Zoroaster, also known as Zarathustra. He may have lived around 600 B.C.E., or as long ago as 1800 B.C.E. The stories about his childhood are full of miracles. They say that he was born laughing and that wild animals saved his life several times. About 150 000 people practice the religion today. A few Zoroastrians live in Iran, but the largest number live in India, where they are called Parsees (after Persia, the former name of Iran).

TEACHINGS AND BELIEFS

The religion teaches that Ahura Mazda, the supreme God, is the creator of the universe and the source of all light. He created all the good in the world, but he constantly struggles against an evil force. Zoroastrians believe that, in the end, good will overcome evil. People are urged to practice good thoughts, good words and good deeds.

Zoroastrianism shares many beliefs with Judaism, Christianity and Islam. These include beliefs in angels, heaven and hell, God and Satan, the resurrection of the body, life everlasting and the Last Judgment.

The most sacred symbol is fire. Like the sun, fire represents purity, light, power and warmth. Zoroastrians keep a pot of fire burning in every household. All prayers and rituals must take place in the presence of fire.

MARKING SPECIAL EVENTS

Boys and girls join the Zoroastrian religion in a special ceremony. A woolen cord is wrapped three times around their waist. They will tie and untie the cord during prayers, which Zoroastrians say five times a day.

Weddings take place in the evening, shortly after sunset. Just as light and darkness come together at twilight, the bride and groom unite to share their lives.

THE LAST JUDGMENT

Zoroastrians believe that after people die their souls are allowed three days to think about their past life. The souls are then judged by God and sent across a bridge to heaven or down to hell. In the end, however, goodness will triumph over evil and even those in hell will be freed.

After a person dies, Zoroastrians place the body in a "Tower of Silence" open to the sky. There, birds such as vultures feed on the flesh.

At a seven-year-old's initiation ceremony, a sacred cord is wrapped around the waist.

QUICK FACTS

Followers: *175 000*

Locations: *Iran, India*

God: *Ahura Mazda*

Teacher/Founder: *Zoroaster*

Scripture: *Avesta*

Places of worship: *fire temples*

Religious leaders: *priests*

Major festivals: *New Year, Sada (Fire Festival), Birthday of Zoroaster*

BAHA'I

One of the world's newest religions, Baha'i (pronounced bah-HIGH) began about 150 years ago in Persia, now Iran. A man who called himself the Bab, meaning the gateway to God, predicted the coming of a new prophet. His teachings were opposed by Islam. But the religion grew through the ideas of the Bab's disciple, Baha'u'llah, whose title means the glory of God. In 1863 C.E., in the garden of Ridvan near Baghdad, Baha'u'llah announced to his followers that he was the prophet foretold by the Bab. The religion has now spread to many continents, including North America.

TEACHINGS AND BELIEFS

Followers of the Baha'i faith believe that there is one God for all people, and that all people and all religions are one. Baha'i prophets include Abraham, Moses, Jesus, Buddha and Muhammad. The goals of the religion are to preach the oneness of all humanity and to promote world peace.

As members of a modern religion, Baha'is believe that science and religion can be unified. They also believe men and women of all races are equal members of one human family.

The Shrine of the Bab in Haifa, Israel, is a Baha'i temple.

QUICK FACTS

Followers: 7.7 million

Locations: Israel, worldwide

God: one God

Teachers/Founders: the Bab and Baha'u'llah

Scriptures: writings of the Bab and Baha'u'llah

Places of worship: homes and temples

Religious leaders: any educated member

Major festivals: Feast of Ridvan, Birthday of the Bab

WORSHIP

Baha'is usually worship in one another's homes. They have no religious leaders. Respected members of the community conduct the worship services and read from the scriptures. Baha'is also pray every day.

The Baha'is have built several magnificent temples around the world. Each temple is surrounded by beautiful gardens with fountains, as Baha'u'llah instructed. Most are nine-sided (nine stands for unity) and have large domes.

FESTIVALS

The twelve-day Feast of Ridvan commemorates the Baha'u'llah's announcement in the garden. Baha'is celebrate the New Year on March 21, the first day of spring, with picnics and music. Another festival takes place on the birthday of the Bab.

TAOISM

About 2500 years ago, China was a country with many problems. Many different philosophies arose, proposing ways to restore peace and harmony. Two of them — Taoism and Confucianism — became very popular. Confucianism taught people how to behave correctly toward other people. Taoism was concerned more with the individual, offering ways to ensure health and well-being. The founder of Taoism was Lao Tzu.

THE LIFE OF LAO TZU

The name "Lao Tzu" means Old Master or Old Wise Person. Lao Tzu is said to have lived about 500 B.C.E., at the same time as Confucius and the Buddha. He was a librarian in the royal court of China. Many people listened to his wise advice, but he didn't write down any of his teachings.

Finally, when he was very old, Lao Tzu became unhappy at the conflict he saw around him and went on a journey to the west. At the Chinese border, a guard asked him to write down his thoughts. He agreed,

Lao Tzu, the founder of Taoism, rides on a buffalo.

but wrote only about five thousand characters (each Chinese character is one word). His short book became known as the Tao Te Ching, meaning The Way and Its Power.

TEACHINGS AND BELIEFS

"Tao" means the way or the path, but it is a very hard idea to put into words. Tao has no form, no beginning and no end. It is the energy or power that flows through all things.

The goal of a Taoist is to become one with the Tao and to allow the Tao to be free. To do this, a person must learn to let things happen (this is called *wu wei*, or inaction). Inaction does not mean doing nothing; it means letting things happen as they do in nature, or acting without scheming. It also means giving up the desire for possessions and for control. Long life and immortality are other goals that Taoists pursue, using meditation and physical exercises.

Some Taoists believe in Gods and Goddesses and include them in their religion. Some of these Gods are similar to those of ancient Chinese folk religions. They are supposed to bring health, wealth or long life. Other Gods rule heaven and watch what people do.

This symbol represents yin and yang, two opposite forces that work together in all things. Yin is dark and heavy and bound to the earth. Yang is light and airy. The dot of one inside the other shows that there is the seed of each in the other.

QUICK FACTS

Followers: *numbers not available*

Locations: *China and elsewhere in Asia*

Gods: *Gods and Goddesses*

Teacher/Founder: *Lao Tzu*

Scriptures: *Tao Te Ching, Chuang Tzu*

Places of worship: *temples*

Religious leaders: *priests, monks, nuns*

Major festivals: *New Year, Ching Ming, Hungry Ghost*

The Tao

"Stand before it — there is no beginning.
Follow it and there is no end.
Stay with the Tao. Move with the present."

— *from the Tao Te Ching*

SCRIPTURES

The two main Taoist books are the Tao Te Ching and the Chuang Tzu. The Tao Te Ching is written in the form of poems. It teaches rulers how to live in a way that brings about harmony to their country.

The writings of Chuang Tzu, a Chinese philosopher who lived from 399 to 295 B.C.E., are also important to Taoism. The Chuang Tzu (named after the writer) contains parables and conversations about how to meditate, what to eat and how to live. It tells stories of beings called Immortals, people who live forever. Some believe these are the models that people should follow.

Hsi-Wang-Mu, Queen Mother of the West, reigns over the Eight Immortals.

For Taoists, nature is both beautiful and sacred. Mountains like these, on the banks of the Li River, are symbols of immortality.

How Do You Say These Names?

Tao and ***Taoism*** Tao is pronounced Dow to rhyme with cow. Taoism is pronounced DOW-ism. Taoism is sometimes spelled Daoism.
Lao Tzu Lao is pronounced Low to rhyme with cow. Tzu is pronounced Dzuh. Lao Tzu is sometimes spelled Laozi.
Chuang Tzu Chuang is pronounced Jwang. Tzu is pronounced Dzuh. His name is sometimes spelled Zhuangzi.
Tao Te Ching Tao is pronounced Dow to rhyme with cow. Te Ching is pronounced Duh Jing.

RELIGIOUS WAYS

Taoism is a very personal religion. Taoists practice meditation, chanting and exercise as ways of improving their inner balance and attaining good health and long life. *Tai chi* (pronounced tie-jee), a set of exercises based on martial-arts moves, helps to improve the flow of energy. Acupuncture is also thought to have developed from Taoism. It is said to remove blocks from the paths of energy in the body.

Taoist religious services seek to achieve harmony between heaven and earth and between yin and yang.

Taoists consider a proper burial especially important to ensure that the soul is at peace.

The flowing movements of tai chi help balance yin and yang.

CONFUCIANISM

K'ung Fu Tzu (pronounced kung FOO dzuh), whom Westerners call Confucius, taught people to live well and behave properly toward each other. He believed that if people acted with generosity and respect, there would be peace and harmony in the country.

Confucius did not seek to found a religion. But he did accept some of the ideas of the older Chinese religions, such as ancestor worship. After he died, his followers set up temples in his honor.

Confucius taught people to live well and to respect their ancestors.

THE LIFE OF CONFUCIUS

Confucius, whose Chinese name means Master Kung, was born in 551 B.C.E. in northern China, the youngest of eleven children in a rich family. His elderly father died soon after the birth of Confucius, and the family lost its wealth. Confucius studied hard, however, and in his late teens he got a job working for the government.

Over the next thirty years, Confucius carried on this work and also began to teach. In his fifties, he left his job to wander and instruct others. Eventually, he returned and continued to teach, to write and to advise political leaders. By the time he died in 479 B.C.E., he had three thousand students.

Those who came after Confucius changed and added to his philosophy. Meng Tzu (pronounced MUNG dzuh), called Mencius by Westerners, was a teacher like Confucius. He taught that people were basically good and that they do the right things naturally.

Another follower of Confucius was Hsun Tzu (pronounced SHUN dzuh). He thought that people were born evil and had to work hard to overcome their greedy natures.

Later rulers of China used Confucian ideas as the basis for government and law.

QUICK FACTS

Followers: *numbers not available*

Locations: *China, Taiwan, Korea, Japan, Vietnam, Singapore*

Teacher/Founder: *K'ung Fu Tzu (Confucius)*

Scriptures: *the Five Classics, the Four Books*

Places of worship: *temples dedicated to Confucius*

Major festivals: *New Year, Ching Ming, Hungry Ghost*

Every year, the Chinese emperor came to the Temple of Heaven in Beijing, China, to pray for a good harvest. The temple (fifteenth century C.E.) reflects Confucius' ideas about the balance between heaven and earth.

TEACHINGS AND BELIEFS

Confucius taught people to behave well toward each other. Proper social behavior (called *li*), he said, would create an ideal society. To be polite, generous and respectful, people need *jen* (pronounced run), an inner goodness. Kindness to others, said Confucius, means doing for others what you would like them to do for you.

Five Relationships

Confucius described five relationships that can exist between people:

- Husband — wife
- Father — son
- Ruler — ministers and subjects
- Older brother — younger brother
- Older friend — younger friend

He explained that in each relationship the senior person should act with kindness toward the junior person, who should in turn respect and obey the senior one.

Men predict the future by matching stick patterns with the I Ching.

SCRIPTURES

The Five Classics

Followers of Confucius were encouraged to study the Five Classics.

1. The Book of Changes (I Ching) is an ancient book used to tell the future. It contains sixty-four diagrams, each with six lines. Some lines are solid and some are broken. A person throws coins or sticks to make a diagram that tells the future. This book continues to fascinate people today.
2. The Book of History (Shu Ching) is a book of historical events.
3. The Book of Poetry (Shih Ching) is a book of three hundred poems or songs about everyday events and things.
4. The Book of Rites (Li Chi) is a book of rituals, including many to be performed out of respect for the dead.
5. Spring and Autumn Annals (Ch'un Ch'iu) tells of events before and after Confucius lived.

Women light sticks of incense at a Confucian shrine in Vietnam.

The Four Books

For centuries, students who wanted jobs in the Chinese government had to memorize the Five Classics. Long after Confucius died, Four Books were added to their study list. They are:

1. The Analects, a book that records the words of Confucius himself.
2. The Book of Great Learning, which tells how a gentleman should act.
3. The Doctrine of the Mean, a book that encourages self-control.
4. Mencius, the teachings of Mencius.

RELIGIOUS WAYS

Confucianism has no clergy, but it does have ceremonies and rituals. Confucius said these ceremonies link people with heaven and earth and their ancestors. They also help people to live together in harmony.

In ancient China, temples were built to honor Confucius. Initially, they contained statues of Confucius, but in 1503 C.E. the statues were removed, and only tablets with his writings remained.

Confucius encouraged the ancient Chinese belief that the emperors were the Sons of Heaven. This belief ended when the last emperor died, early in the twentieth century. When the Communists took over in 1949, Confucianism, along with other religions, was discouraged.

CHINESE CEREMONIES AND FESTIVALS

Before Taoism and Confucianism began, Chinese people believed in folk religions. They asked various Gods and Goddesses for a good harvest, for wealth or for good health. These folk religions survived and mixed in with the newer religions.

In about 100 C.E., Buddhism came to China, where it was adopted and changed by the Chinese. Taoism, Confucianism, Buddhism and folk religions all continued to influence one another. As a result, many Chinese ceremonies and festivals belong to more than one religion.

CEREMONIES
Childhood

All children are taught to respect their elders and to be kind and virtuous. They learn that it is their special duty to care for their elderly parents and in-laws when they grow up.

Between ages fifteen and twenty, boys and girls are welcomed as adults. In the initiation ceremony, an adult places a cap on a boy's head or a pin on a girl's hair. The boy or girl then puts on the clothes of an adult and receives his or her adult name.

Weddings

At her wedding, a woman leaves her family and becomes a part of her husband's family. The groom takes her in a carriage from her house to his home. The couple then exchange cups of wine to mark their marriage.

Funerals

Traditionally, the ceremonies surrounding a death are long and complicated. After the body is washed and dressed, it is placed in a coffin. Every day, people bring food. After three months, they bury the body along with food and gifts. They believe that part of the soul remains with the body and part goes to heaven. After the burial, the person's name is added to that of the ancestors.

A classical Chinese garden reminds people of the need for beauty, peace and harmony in the middle of their busy lives.

Ancestor Worship

Respect for the dead, or ancestor worship, began before the time of Confucius and continued afterwards. Families keep a place of honor, sometimes a whole room, where the names of their dead ancestors are written. The oldest man in the family is responsible for keeping their memory alive.

At a funeral, paper "money" is burned as an offering to the Gods.

FESTIVALS

New Year's Festival

Chinese New Year starts with the new moon at the end of January or beginning of February and lasts for many days. Families gather and give gifts. Children receive money in red paper envelopes. At a parade, a huge dragon puppet with many people inside winds along the streets. The dragon represents long life. Firecrackers frighten away evil spirits.

At New Year, some people believe, the kitchen God goes to heaven and reports to the Jade Emperor, the ruler of heaven, on each family's actions during the past year. To make the kitchen God's words sweet, people rub the lips of a paper statue with honey. They burn the statue in hopes that the God will rise to heaven and say good things about them. Then they replace the old statue with a new one.

A New Year's dragon parade winds through the streets of Hong Kong.

Ching Ming

At Ching Ming, which usually occurs in early April, people make a springtime visit to the home of their parents or grandparents. They clean the family burial place and make fresh offerings to their ancestors.

Dragon boat racers pull on the oars to the rhythm of the drum.

Hungry Ghost Festival

On the seventh day of the seventh lunar month (in August or September), it is said that the lost and hungry souls are released from hell and roam the earth. People put out food for these ghosts to keep them out of their houses. They light lanterns to help the ghosts find the food, and they burn paper money for the ghosts to spend. Plays and musical events entertain the ghosts to keep them from causing trouble.

Dragon Boat Festival

At the Dragon Boat Festival in June, people all over the world race boats that have the head and tail of a dragon. The festival commemorates the actions of a poet named Chu Yuan and the people who tried to save him.

Chu Yuan was a good man who lived more than two thousand years ago. Unable to convince the emperor to act honestly, he jumped into a river and drowned. Many people tried to save him, but his body was never found. According to the story, it was eaten by dragons.

SHINTO

 Shinto is the ancient religion of Japan — at least 1500 years old. "Shinto" means way of the Gods. Today, many Japanese people combine Shinto rituals with other religions, especially Buddhism. Shinto and Buddhism both became official religions of Japan in about 700 C.E.

WORSHIP

According to Shinto, nature is full of spirits, called *kami*. People worship kami and ask them for favors at shrines and at home. Shrines can be large or small, but all have one or more gates, called *torii* (meaning bird). These gates represent the line between the everyday world and the spiritual world. People bow as they pass through the torii. As they enter a shrine, people clap their hands to get the kami's attention.

Shinto priests bang drums close to the shrine of the kami. This is another way to alert the kami to the presence of worshipers.

Many shrines have mirrors representing the Sun Goddess, Amaterasu. According to the legend, when the Sun Goddess departed from Earth, she left a mirror behind to represent herself. Shinto teaches that the Sun Goddess is the ancestor of the Japanese emperor's family and of all the Japanese people.

SCRIPTURES

The two ancient books of Shinto are the Kojiki and the Nihongi. They tell a creation story in which heaven and earth were once one substance. Then a reed sprang up and separated them. This reed became the first kami. Later, the first male and female kami came into being. This couple descended to the islands of Japan and gave birth to numerous kami offspring.

A Shinto priest beats a drum to rouse the spirits.

QUICK FACTS

Followers: 4 million or more

Location: Japan

Gods: Amaterasu (the Sun Goddess), kami (spirits)

Scriptures: Kojiki, Nihongi

Places of worship: shrines

Religious leaders: priests

Major festivals: New Year, Hinamatsuri, Children's Day

This red torii (gate to a Shinto shrine) rises from the sea near Miyajima Island, Japan.

On Children's Day, a boy helps attach carp kites to a pole.

MARKING SPECIAL EVENTS

There are Four Affirmations in Shinto: tradition and family, love of nature, physical cleanliness, and the worship of ancestors. Special ceremonies help people to reach these ideals.

Childhood

Children have their own ceremonies. Newborn babies are registered at a Shinto shrine. At the Seven-Five-Three Festival (Shichigosan) on November 15, girls who are three and seven years old and boys who are five years old thank the kami for looking after them. On Adults' Day, January 15, young people who have reached the age of twenty celebrate their adulthood. The women receive a silk kimono.

Weddings and Funerals

Weddings in Japan are usually Shinto ceremonies, but most funerals are conducted by Buddhist priests. Homes often contain both a Shinto altar for the kami and the Sun Goddess and a Buddhist altar to honor the ancestors.

FESTIVALS

Festivals are held around the year. Often featuring colorful parades, they are an important part of Japanese life.

Hinamatsuri

Hinamatsuri takes place on March 3. On this day, mothers and daughters arrange beautifully dressed dolls on shelves, with the emperor and empress on the top.

Children's Day

Children's Day comes on May 5. Families hang paper carp one below the other to represent the sons, and sometimes daughters, in the family.

In a Tokyo park, children enjoy a picnic under the blossoming cherry trees.

Cherry Blossom

The most famous Japanese festival is the Cherry Blossom Festival in early spring. Families and friends bring picnics and sit under the flowering trees.

New Year's Day

One of the biggest festivals is New Year's Day, or Shogatsu. Millions of people crowd into the shrines to ask for the blessings of the kami in the coming year. They eat special rice cakes and decorate their homes with flowers, pine branches, bamboo, straw and white paper.

O-Bon

At the festival of the dead, called O-Bon, the souls of the ancestors are supposed to return to their homes. Families gather to entertain them, feed them and light farewell bonfires.

Mount Fuji is sacred to many Japanese as a home of the Gods.

RELIGIONS FROM AFRICA

Today, many Africans are Christian or Muslim, but ancient African beliefs still exist. Although each African tribe has its own beliefs and rituals, most African religions tell a story about how the earth and everything in it began. The Dogon people, for example, believe that the chief God created the sun and the moon in the form of pots. He gave the sun red rings and the moon white rings. To create the stars, he flung bits of pots into the sky. The earth, he created from a lump of clay.

In African religions, one God usually rules over many other spirits. Nature spirits are invisible but all around, often dwelling in sacred places such as mountaintops and rivers. Ancestor spirits try to protect their living relatives. Trickster Gods, such as Anansi the spider, or the tortoise of the Yoruba people of Nigeria, do surprising things. They often upset the plans of spirits or people.

Some people are believed to have special powers. They can talk to the spirits or even enter the world of the spirits while in a trance.

MARKING SPECIAL EVENTS

Birth and marriage ceremonies are joyful occasions for African people. Initiation ceremonies, which mark a child's membership in the group, are important, too. Funerals help the dead person to pass from this world to the world of spirits and ancestors.

Belonging to a group or village means taking care of each other and doing things that are good for all. There is an African saying, "It takes a village to raise a child."

AFRO-CARIBBEAN RELIGIONS

Several hundred years ago, many African men and women were captured and taken from their homes to be slaves in the Caribbean islands. These people brought their African religions with them. They often combined their beliefs and rituals with Christianity and local Caribbean religions. Some of these mixed religions are still practiced today. Three examples are Voudou, in Haiti; Santeria, in Cuba; and Macumba, in Brazil.

This mask from Cameroon, in Africa, represents a forest spirit.

Wearing ritual masks and costumes, Dogon dancers leap into the air.

RELIGIONS FROM NORTH AMERICA

There are many different nations among the Indigenous Peoples — Native Americans, First Nations, Métis and Inuit — in North America. Some of their religions have changed over time, but many traditions and beliefs continue. There are differences, but also similarities, in the beliefs of the various nations. Most believe in a Creator, sometimes called Great Spirit or Great Mystery, and in good spirits who help people by bringing good hunting or plentiful crops, for example.

Spiritual beliefs are not a separate part of life for Indigenous Peoples. The spirit world teaches them how to gather or kill their food and guides them in their understanding of nature. The goal of human life is to be in harmony with both the natural and the supernatural world.

TEACHINGS AND BELIEFS

Animals play a big part in North American Indigenous stories. The Haudenosaunee and Algonquian Nations tell this creation story: Our world began when Skywoman fell from the sky. Birds flew up to help bring her safely to Earth, and a giant turtle rose to the ocean's surface to give her a place to land. Then a muskrat dived to the bottom of the sea, brought up a paw full of mud and placed it on the turtle's back. This bit of earth grew into Turtle Island, the name Indigenous Peoples use for what is now known as North America.

Many stories tell of trickster spirits such as Coyote (in the American Southwest) or Raven (in the Pacific Northwest). Tricksters often bring people presents such as fire for cooking, or special skills such as weaving or growing corn.

Some members of a nation are specially trained in medicines and spirituality. They help guide their people with their sacred knowledge and abilities.

MARKING SPECIAL EVENTS

Ceremonies celebrate the stages of life — birth, marriage, old age and death. The people chant, play drums and dance, hoping to strengthen the group and bring it good fortune. Masks and costumes are important in dancing ceremonies.

In some nations, people go on journeys, sometimes called vision quests, to receive sacred knowledge and spiritual guidance.

Some Indigenous Peoples on the Pacific Northwest coast carve tall wooden totem poles. The totems, or images, represent animals, ancestors and spirits.

The sacred pipe plays a role in many Indigenous North American ceremonies. It can welcome guests or seal a peace treaty.

RELIGIONS FROM AUSTRALIA

Indigenous Australian peoples have lived in Australia for thousands of years. They believe that long ago, in a time called Dreamtime, amazing creatures, human and animal, roamed their land. The things that these creatures did left marks on nature — for example, an enormous footprint created a valley.

Indigenous Australian peoples paint pictures of Dreamtime and act out the stories in their ceremonies, called *corroborees*. They try to "break through" to Dreamtime with art and music and walkabouts.

Special ceremonies mark the time when young people become adults.

Uluru is a sacred site to the Indigenous Australian peoples.

At a corroboree, Indigenous Australian peoples celebrate Dreamtime with dancing, music and story-telling. The man on the right is playing a didjeridu.

In an Indigenous Australian painting, giant snakes encircle the creatures in a Dreamtime landscape.

GLOSSARY

afterlife   a life that follows death

baptism   a ceremony using water as a sign that a child or adult is admitted into a Christian church

church   a building for Christian worship; a community of Christians

circumcision   the removal of the foreskin of the penis

clergy   the leaders of a religion who perform rituals and teach

commemorate   to honor the memory of a person or event

congregation   group of people gathered for worship; members of a church or synagogue

covenant   an agreement between humans and a deity

cremation   burning a dead body to ashes

deity   a God or Goddess

divine   of a deity; sacred

divine being   a God or Goddess

faith   belief and trust in a deity or a religion

fast   to eat little or no food

God   a supreme being with supernatural powers

grace   the love, blessing and protection of a deity

gurdwara   a Sikh place of worship

heaven   a happy place where good souls live

hell   a place where wicked souls are punished

holy   sacred, connected to a deity

hymn   a song that praises or thanks a deity

idol   a picture or statue that is worshiped as a deity

immortal   living forever

incense   the source of sweet-smelling smoke used in worship

initiation   a ceremony to admit a person to a group

mantra   a word or phrase that people repeat as part of worship or meditation

meditation   sitting very still and focusing one's thoughts

miracle   a wonderful event that cannot be explained

monk   a man who belongs to a religious community and lives a life of prayer, meditation and service

monotheism   the belief that there is only one God

mosque   a building for Muslim worship

nun   a woman who belongs to a religious community and lives a life of prayer, meditation and service

parable   a story with a message about life or religion

persecute   treat badly, especially for religious or political reasons

philosophy   a set of ideas about life or the universe

pilgrimage   a trip to a sacred place, especially for religious reasons

practice   religious rituals; to follow a religion

prayer   words or thoughts addressed to a deity

prophet   a person who is believed to speak with the words of a deity

reincarnation   a rebirth of the soul in a new body

ritual   a religious ceremony

sacrament   a ritual that represents the grace of a deity

sacred   holy, connected to a deity

sacrifice   something offered to a deity, often an animal that has been killed

scripture   a sacred or religious book

sermon   a talk about religion, usually as part of a worship service

service   a religious meeting for purposes of worship

sin   a bad action that offends a deity

soul   a part of a person separate from the body

spirit   a supernatural being

spiritual   sacred or religious; interested in things of the spirit

supernatural   beyond the laws of nature

symbol   an object, animal or person that stands for an idea

synagogue   a building for Jewish worship

temple   a building dedicated to worship

tradition   a way of thinking or acting that is passed from one generation to the next

worship   ceremonies for showing love and honor to a deity

INDEX